The UK

Air Fryer

Recipe Book

Easy, Fuss-Free and Delicious Traditional British Recipes Using European Measurement and UK Ingredients

Introduction

Enjoy guilt-free air fried favourites, or bake and roast delicious meals all in one convenient appliance. Whatever your craving, The UK Air Fryer Recipe Book for Beginner is the perfect guide to get started.

This recipe book will teach you not only how to use your air fryer, but also the basics of cooking from scratch in your new favourite kitchen appliance. Learn how to use an air fryer to make the juiciest meats, crispiest chips, and perfect vegetable sides with little to no oil and no cleanup!

AIR FRYER 101

Do you know how to use your new air fryer? I'll walk you through everything you need to know to get started with this versatile kitchen appliance in this beginner's guide. What you can cook in an air fryer, how to use an air fryer, safety precautions, cleaning your air fryer, and the best air fryer recipes to get most of your air fryer.

"An air fryer can help you prepare quick, healthy, and delicious meals. It has the incredible ability to crisp up foods while using very little oil. Proteins are especially tender and juicy when cooked. When it's hot outside, use an air fryer instead of your oven to cook without overheating your kitchen ."

WHAT CAN YOU COOK IN AN AIR FRYER

In an air fryer, you can cook almost anything! Proteins such as chicken, fish, or beef, as well as healthy vegetable side dishes, appetisers such as courgette chips and even desserts and baked goods.

The air fryer is ideal for cooking foods that require a high level of crispiness or crunch, such as French fries, fried chicken, and baked potatoes with crispy skins. It's also one of my favourite ways to cook meats like steak or chicken because it always results in juicy, flavorful results.

HOW DOES AN AIR FRYER WORK

A heating element radiates heat from an air fryer, and a fan circulates hot air around the food in the air fryer basket. Because of the hot air circulation, you can use much less oil than you would in the oven while still getting the crispy foods you crave.

AIR FRYER SAFETY PRECAUTIONS

It is absolutely important to read and follow all of the safety precautions included in the manual for your air fryer. Here are some simple tips on how to use your air fryer safely:

- An air fryer is designed for air frying rather than traditional oil frying, and the basket should never be filled with oil.

- Cook in a well-ventilated area at all times. Allow enough space around the air fryer for the exhaust to circulate.

- Keep in mind the smoke point of the cooking oils you use. It might be best to avoid using oils with low smoke points or to cook at a lower temperature. Oils should not smoke, burn, or splatter on the heating element.

- After using the air fryer, keep your hands and countertops safe from the hot basket. When removing the hot basket from the air fryer, place it on a silicone trivet or pot holder/hot pad.

- Unplug the air fryer when it is not in use.

- Never set your air fryer on the hop.

- Fill the basket only halfway. Food should always be cooked in a single layer in the air fryer basket, not layered, to ensure crispness and even cooking. You can cook in batches if necessary.

- It is acceptable to remove the basket during the cooking cycle to check on the progress of your food.

- To make foods crispy, dry them thoroughly. Pat food dry with a clean kitchen towel or paper towels before adding oil, seasonings, or placing it in the air fryer basket.

- Do not use perforated baking paper at high temperatures unless it is covered with food. If there isn't enough food to weigh down the baking paper, it will fly around and cover the food as the hot air circulates. This causes the food to cook unevenly. Also, if the parchment is flying around and collides with the hot heating element, it may catch fire.

- While the food is in the air fryer, do not season it with salt. Laying dry salt on nonstick interiors may cause the basket coating to peel. Season the food in a bowl or chopping board first, then place it in the air fryer. Alternatively, season after cooking.

- Keep in mind that the outside of your air fryer is extremely hot (especially the back). Do not touch it!

- Grease the basket of your Air Fryer. Even if your food does not require oil, it is always a good idea to grease your air fryer basket. grease by rubbing or spraying some oil onto the bottom grates. This will prevent your food from sticking.

- Never use aerosol spray cans in your air fryer

HOW TO USE AN AIR FRYER.

1. Before you begin cooking in the air fryer, it must be preheated. This is due to the fact that when you preheat the air fryer, the food cooks at a higher temperature and has a crispy exterior.

2. When the air fryer has finished preheating, remove the air fryer basket and place the food in the basket.

3. Insert the air fryer basket into the air fryer after it has been filled with food.
Then, set the time and temperature.

4. To begin air frying, press the start button. To ensure that the food is fully cooked, mix the contents in the middle of the cooking process or flip the food upside down. The air fryer will make a beeping sound when the cooking time is up.

5. Remove the air fryer basket. But be cautious of the hot steam. Serve the food. keep the basket on a flat surface. Before cleaning, the basket must be completely cool.

NOW IT'S TIME TO GET COOKING! TO GET YOU STARTED, HERE ARE SOME DELICIOUS AIR FRYER RECIPES.

———

Breakfast

Snacks & Sides

Beef

Poultry

Seafood

Desserts

Scrambled Eggs

Prep Time
3 Minutes

Cook Time
9 Minutes

Total Time
12 Minutes

Serving Size
4 servings

INGREDIENTS

- 3tablespoon unsalted butter, melted
- 2 eggs
- 2 tablespoons milk
- 50g cheddar cheese
- Salt & pepper to taste

Steps

1. In a bowl, add eggs, milk, salt & pepper. Whisk until combined.
2. In a baking tin that will fit in your air fryer. Add butter & eggs. Place tin in air fryer basket.
3. Air Fry at 300˚F/150˚C for 3 mins.
4. Remove tin from air fryer then push eggs to the inside of the tin to stir them around. Air Fry for 2 mins then add cheese, stir. Air Fry 2 more minutes.
5. Remove tin from air fryer and serve immediately.

Egg in a Hole

Prep Time
5 Minutes

Cook Time
8 Minutes

Total Time
13 Minutes

Serving Size
1 servings

INGREDIENTS

- 1 slice of your favorite bread
- 1 tablespoon melted butter
- 1 egg
- Salt and pepper to taste

Steps

1. Preheat air fryer to 162°C/325°F.
2. Brush both sides of bread with butter. Cut a hole in center of the bread. Crack the egg into the middle of the bread. Transfer to a greased air fryer basket.
3. Air Fry for 6 mins. Flip and air fry for 2 more minutes.
4. Season with salt and pepper and serve.

8

Poached Eggs

Prep Time
5 Minutes

Cook Time
5 Minutes

Total Time
10 Minutes

Serving Size
4 servings

INGREDIENTS

- 4 eggs
- 8 tablespoons water
- Salt & pepper to taste

Steps

1. Preheat air fryer to 182°C/360°F.
2. Grease 4 ramekins, crack one egg in each ramekin into it. Add 2 tablespoons water into each ramekin. Place ramekins on air fryer basket
3. Air Fry at 182°C/360°F for 4 mins.
4. Remove ramekins from air fryer, lift the egg from remaining water.
5. Serve.

Breakfast Casserole

Prep Time
15 Minutes

Cook Time
10 Minutes

Total Time
25 Minutes

Serving Size
6 servings

INGREDIENTS

- 500g hash browns
- 500g minced sausage
- 2 red bell pepper, (chopped)
- 50g grated cheddar cheese
- 1 yellow bell pepper, (chopped)
- 1 onion, (chopped)
- 4 eggs
- Salt & pepper to taste

Steps

1. Grease a baking dish that will fit in your air fryer. Add the hash browns on the bottom of the dish. Then top with minced sausage. Add the peppers and onion on top, then sprinkle cheese on top.
2. Air fry at 355˚F/180˚C for 10 mins. Remove dish from air fryer & stir the casserole.
3. In a bowl, whisk eggs then pour right on top of the casserole. Air fry at 355˚F/180˚C for another 10 mins.
4. Serve.

Jacket Potatoes

Prep Time
15 Minutes   Cook Time
30 Minutes   Total Time
45 Minutes   Serving Size
4 servings

INGREDIENTS

- 4 medium potatoes, washed and poked with a fork
- 1 tablespoon oil
- Salt to taste

Steps

1. Preheat air fryer to 205°C/400°F. Rub each potato with oil, then sprinkle with salt.
2. Put them in the air fryer basket (in batches). Air Fry for 30 minutes. Check potato doneness by poking potatoes with fork. If fork does not easily pierce potatoes, return basket to air fryer. Air Fry for another 5 minutes. Repeat until potatoes are ready.
3. Remove basket from air fryer and carefully transfer potatoes to chopping board. Slice potatoes down center.
4. Dress jacket potatoes with desired topping and serve.

Courgette Pizza Boats

Prep Time
5 Minutes   Cook Time
8 Minutes   Total Time
13 Minutes   Serving Size
4 servings

INGREDIENTS

- 2 courgette, (cut lengthwise)
- 60g Pizza Sauce/MARINARA SAUCE
- Mini Pepperoni
- Shredded Mozzarella Cheese
- sliced green olives
- sliced cherry tomato
- Olive Oil Spray

Steps

1. Core the courgette middle out with a spoon. Spray the courgette with cooking spray.
2. Brush the courgette with marinara/pizza sauce, top with pepperoni, olives,tomato and cheese. Put them in the air fryer basket. Coat them with cooking spray.
3. Air fry at 355˚F/180˚C for 8 minutes.

Fish Cakes

Prep Time 12 Minutes **Cook Time** 6 Minutes **Total Time** 18 Minutes **Serving Size** 4 servings

INGREDIENTS

- 500g skinless cod/haddock fillets, chopped
- 250g peeled & grated potatoes
- 4 tbsp plain flour
- 2 tbsp dill & parsley, chopped
- Salt & pepper to taste

Steps

1. In a large bowl, add fish, potatoes, dill and flour. Season with salt & pepper. Mix until combined. Shape into 8 patties, then refrigerate for 30 minutes.
2. Spray air fryer basket with cooking spray. Add patties on basket in a single layer coat with cooking spray.
3. Air Fry at 190°C/375°F for 10 mins. (flipping and spraying with cooking spray halfway through cooking time).

Baked Oats

Prep Time 2 Minutes **Cook Time** 15 Minutes **Total Time** 17 Minutes **Serving Size** 2 servings

INGREDIENTS

- ½ large Banana
- 40g rolled oats
- 1 tbsp maple syrup
- 1 tsp vanilla extract
- ½ tsp baking powder
- 1 Large Egg
- 60g milk of choice
- ½ tsp ground cinnamon or nutmeg
- blueberries or your favorite fruits

Steps

1. Grease 2 ramekins and set aside. Add all ingredients into the blender. Blend till smooth.
2. Add oats mixture to ramekins and top with fruits.
3. Bake in air fryer at 330°F / 165°C for 15 mins.
4. Remove from air fryer add your favorite toppings.

Roasted Cheesy Tomatoes

Prep Time
5 Minutes

Cook Time
3 Minutes

Total Time
8 Minutes

Serving Size
2 servings

INGREDIENTS

- 1-2 tomatoes
- salt & pepper to taste
- 80g grated parmesan
- 120g mozzarella cheese
- 6 fresh basil leaves
- olive oil

Steps

1. Slice the tomatoes into thick slices and place into a greased baking dish that will fit in your air fryer.
2. Top the tomatoes with salt, pepper, grated parmesan cheese, and mozzarella cheese.
3. Cook at 400°F/200°C for 3 minutes.
4. Top with fresh basil and enjoy.

Turkey Breakfast Burgers

Prep Time
10 Minutes

Cook Time
8 Minutes

Total Time
18 Minutes

Serving Size
8 servings

INGREDIENTS

- 2 tbsp oil
- 1kg minced turkey
- 1 tbsp soy sauce
- 1 tbsp brown sugar
- 3 tbsp scallions, minced
- 4 garlic cloves, minced
- Salt & pepper to taste

Steps

1. In a bowl, add all ingredients. Mix.
2. Form mixture into 12 patties and flatten between two hands.
3. Spray air fryer basket with cooking spray. Add turkey patties into the basket. Air Fry at 200°C/400°F for 8 minutes, (flipping halfway through cooking time).

Stuffed Peppers

Prep Time 10 *Minutes* **Cook Time** 15 *Minutes* **Total Time** 20 *Minutes* **Serving Size** 4 *servings*

INGREDIENTS

- 4-6 Bell Peppers destemmed and seeds removed
- 400g diced tomatoes
- 400g tomato sauce
- 200g cooked rice
- 1 can black beans drained and rinsed
- 1-2 tsp Italian Seasoning
- 50g mozzarella cheese
- 1 tbsp parmesan cheese

Steps

1. Mix diced tomatoes, tomato sauce, rice, beans and seasoning together.
2. Place mixture into scooped out bell peppers. Fill bell peppers to top with mixture.
3. Place stuffed peppers into air fryer basket. Cook at 360°F/180°C. for 12 minutes. Remove from air fryer but keep in basket.
4. Top stuffed peppers with cheese mixture and cook for another 3 minutes .

Fried Rice

Prep Time 10 *Minutes* **Cook Time** 15 *Minutes* **Total Time** 20 *Minutes* **Serving Size** 4 *servings*

INGREDIENTS

- 550g rice cooked and cold
- 180g frozen vegetables (carrots, corn, broccoli, and peas or edamame)
- 50ml soy sauce
- 1 tbsp oil
- 2 eggs scrambled.

Steps

1. into a large mixing bowl, add rice. Add frozen vegetables. add eggs. add soy sauce and oil . Mix until combined.
2. Transfer rice mixture to an oven-safe container.
3. Place container into air fryer basket. Cook for 15 minutes at 360°F/182°C. Stir three times during cook time.
4. Serve warm.

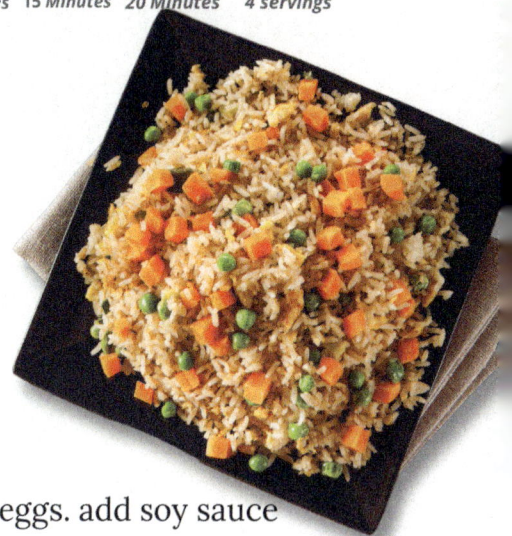

13

Avocado Eggs

Prep Time 12 Minutes **Cook Time** 12 Minutes **Total Time** 24 Minutes **Serving Size** 4 servings

INGREDIENTS

- 2 avocados
- 4 eggs
- 2-4 slices bread

Steps

1. Cut the avocados in half lengthwise. Remove the pit. Carve out some of the avocado flesh.
2. Place parchment paper in the air fryer basket.
3. Place the avocados on top of parchment paper. Place bread slices around the avocados. Crack 1 egg into the cavity of each avocado half. Season with salt and pepper.
4. you can add any additional toppings paprika or parmesan cheese.
5. Cook at 370°F/187°C for 12 minutes or until eggs are done.
6. Remove from the air fryer basket and serve.

Cheesy Baked Eggs

Prep Time 4 Minutes **Cook Time** 16 Minutes **Total Time** 20 Minutes **Serving Size** 2 servings

INGREDIENTS

- 4 large Eggs
- 60g Smoked gouda, chopped
- Everything bagel seasoning
- salt & pepper to taste

Steps

1. Grease the inside of 2 ramekin . Add 2 eggs to each ramekin, then add 30g gouda to each. Salt and pepper to taste. Sprinkle seasoning on top of each ramekin. Stir.
2. Place each ramekin into the air fryer basket. Cook at 400°F/205°C for 16 minutes, or until eggs are cooked through. Serve.

Omelet Frittata

Prep Time
10 Minutes

Cook Time
10 Minutes

Total Time
20 Minutes

Serving Size
2 servings

INGREDIENTS

- 4 Eggs
- 2 tbsp milk
- 1 tomato, sliced
- 2 scallions, chopped
- ½ tsp paprika
- ½ tsp garlic powder
- 50g chicken, beef, sausage
- Salt & pepper to taste

Steps

1. In a large bowl, add eggs then add milk. Whisk until combined. Add chopped spring onions, tomatoes, paprika, garlic powder and season with salt & pepper. Mix.
2. Spray a pan with cooking spray. Pour egg mixture into the baking pan. top with cheese.
3. Put the pan in air fryer basket. Air fry at 185˚F/140˚C for 11 minutes.
4. Remove from air fryer, serve.

Turkey Melt

Prep Time
7 Minutes

Cook Time
8 Minutes

Total Time
15 Minutes

Serving Size
1 servings

INGREDIENTS

- 2 slices bread
- Turkey slices
- 1 tbsp butter
- Sun dried tomato
- Swiss or cheddar cheese slices

Steps

1. Put cheese, sun dried tomato and turkey slices in between bread. Brush outside of bread with butter. Secure with toothpicks.
2. Put sandwich in air fryer basket.
3. Air Fry at 365°F/185°C for 5 minutes to melt the cheese.
4. Flip and air fry another 3 minutes.

Puffed Pancake

Prep Time
5 Minutes

Cook Time
20 Minutes

Total Time
30 Minutes

Serving Size
3 servings

INGREDIENTS

- 3 large eggs
- 60g plain flour
- 120ml milk
- 1 teaspoons vanilla essence
- 2 tablespoons butter

Steps

1. Preheat air fryer to 205°C/400°F. Place a 15-cm cake tin in air fryer while it is preheating.
2. In a blender, add all ingredients (except butter) and blend until smooth.
3. Remove cake tin from air fryer, add butter to the hot cake tin and place it back in the air fryer until melted and bubbly, pour pancake batter into the tin and Air Fry for 18/20 mins.
4. Serve topped with your favorite toppings.

Eggy Bread

Prep Time
6 Minutes

Cook Time
8 Minutes

Total Time
14 Minutes

Serving Size
4 servings

INGREDIENTS

- 2 eggs
- 2 double cream
- ½ teaspoon ground cinnamon
- ½ teaspoon vanilla essence
- 1 loaf brioche bread, cut into 8 thick slices

Steps

1. In a bowl, add egg, milk, vanilla, and cinnamon, whisk and set aside.
2. Spray the air fryer basket with cooking spray
3. Dip bread slices into egg mixture (coat both sides). Allow to drip for a few seconds, then place into the air fryer basket. Repeat with remaining slices
4. Air Fry at 205°C/400°F for 5 minutes. Open basket and flip bread slices. Close the air fryer Air Fry 3 more minutes.
5. Serve with warm maple syrup and powdered sugar or your favorite toppings!

Egg Rolls

Prep Time 20 Minutes   Cook Time 12 Minutes   Total Time 32 Minutes   Serving Size 12 servings

INGREDIENTS

- 2 tbsp oil
- 1 garlic clove, minced
- 1/2 tsp fresh grated ginger
- 1 celery stalk, chopped
- 225g minced chicken
- 3 tbsp oyster sauce
- 1 tbsp soy sauce
- 1 tsp sesame oil
- 1 tbsp sriracha
- 1 chopped scallion
- 12 egg roll wrappers

Steps

1. Heat oil in a pan and saute fry garlic, ginger, celery till fragrant. Add the minced chicken, oyster sauce, s oy sauce, sesame oil, sriracha. cook for 4 minutes. Once chicken is cooked, stir in scallions, remove from heat.
2. place egg roll wrapper. Place a tbsp of filling in the bottom half and wrap corner over the filling. turn both sides over the wrapper and then continue rolling like a burrito. Seal edges with water/beaten egg.
3. Spray air fryer basket with cooking spray. Place egg rolls in basket and spray tops of egg rolls with cooking spray. Cook at 400°F/200°C for 6 minutes. Then flip the egg rolls and cook for an additional 6 minutes.

Vegetable Quesadilla

Prep Time 10 Minutes   Cook Time 5 Minutes   Total Time 15 Minutes   Serving Size 4 servings

INGREDIENTS

- 8 medium flour tortillas
- 100g shredded cheddar cheese
- 1 red bell pepper, chopped
- ½ onion, chopped
- 1 tin black beans, rinsed & drained
- 1 tin corn kernels, rinsed & drained

Steps

1. Place the veggies in the air fryer basket. Spray with oil. Air Fry at 380°F/193°C for 5 minutes.
2. Layer each tortilla with cheese, veggies, and black beans. Fold in half.
3. Secure. Place in the air fryer basket and keep the quesadillas secure by using toothpicks.
4. Air fry for 370°F/187°C for 5 minutes until crispy.

Crescent Breakfast Pockets

Prep Time 10 *Minutes* Cook Time 10 *Minutes* Total Time 20 *Minutes* Serving Size 8 *servings*

INGREDIENTS

- 240g packages refrigerated crescent rolls
- 240g chicken sausage, sliced
- 1 tbsp butter
- 4 large eggs
- salt & pepper to taste
- 80g grated Cheddar cheese

Steps

1. Preheat air fryer to 350°F/176°C.
2. Unroll crescent dough and separate into 16 triangles.
3. Melt butter in a large frying pan over medium-high heat. Add eggs and sausage pieces and season with salt & pepper. Cook for 2 minutes, stirring, until cooked.
4. Place about 2 tbsp of filling and Cheddar cheese onto 8 of crescent triangles. Place remaining crescents on top of filling. Pinch to seal triangle pockets.
5. Cook in air fryer for 6 minutes until golden brown. Serve immediately.

Sausage Breakfast Casserole

Prep Time 15 *Minutes* Cook Time 10 *Minutes* Total Time 25 *Minutes* Serving Size 6 *servings*

INGREDIENTS

- 500g hash browns
- 500g minced sausage
- 3 bell pepper, chopped
- 1 onion, chopped
- 4 eggs
- Salt & pepper to taste

Steps

1. Line the bottom of air fryer basket with parchment paper.
2. Put hash browns on basket. Then top with minced sausage. Sprinkle pepper and onion on top.
3. Air fry at 355°F/180°C for 10 minutes.
4. Open air fryer & mix up the casserole a bit. Crack eggs in a bowl, whisk then pour right on top of the hash browns/vegetables .
5. Air fry at 355°F/180°C for another 10 minutes.
6. Remove from air fryer. Serve.

Potato Wedges

INGREDIENTS

- 3-4 large russet potatoes
- 60ml olive oil
- 1 tbsp garlic powder
- 1 tbsp Italian seasoning
- Salt & pepper to taste
- 50g grated Parmesan

Steps

1. Cut each potato lengthwise in half. Cut each half into three wedges.
2. In a large bowl add all ingredients. Mix.
3. Add potato wedges into a greased air fryer basket.
4. Air Fry at 390°F/200°C for 15 mins. flip every 5 mins until crispy and golden brown.

Sweet Potato Chips

Prep Time 2 Minutes   Cook Time 15 Minutes   Total Time 17 Minutes   Serving Size 4 servings

INGREDIENTS

- 2 medium sweet potato, peeled & sliced into 1/2 cm thick sticks
- 2 tablespoon oil
- 1/2 tsp garlic powder
- 1/2 tsp paprika
- ⅛ tsp black pepper

Steps

1. Preheat Air Fryer to 193°C/380°F
2. Add all ingredients into a large bowl, mix until all chips coated with oil and seasonings.
3. Air Fry (in batches) for 12 mins (flipping half way through cooking time).
4. Serve with your favorite side dish or sauce.

Falafel

Prep Time
2 Minutes
Cook Time
15 Minutes
Total Time
17 Minutes
Serving Size
4 servings

INGREDIENTS

- 200g dried chickpeas, soaked overnight
- 40g parsley
- 1 onion, chopped
- 2 garlic cloves, minced
- 1 tbsp oil
- 1 tbsp lemon juice
- 1 tbsp ground cumin
- ¼ tsp baking soda
- 1 to 3 tbsp water, if needed
- Salt to taste

Steps

1. Drain chickpeas and transfer along with the remaining ingredients to a food processor; process, adding water as needed, until finely ground and the mixture just holds together. Using about 3 tbsps per patty, shape into 12 patties.
2. Grease air fryer basket. Place the Falafel in a single layer in basket and spray the tops with cooking spray. (you may need to cook in batches.)
3. Air Fry at 375°F / 190°C for 12 mins, flipping them over halfway through and coating the tops with cooking spray .

Roasted Vegetables

Prep Time
10 Minutes
Cook Time
13 Minutes
Total Time
25 Minutes
Serving Size
4 servings

INGREDIENTS

- 1 red pepper, chopped
- 1 medium aubergine, cubed
- 1 onion, chopped
- 1 yellow squash, cubed
- 1 tablespoon oil
- 1 tsp garlic powder
- ½ tsp onion powder
- ½ tsp oregano
- Salt & pepper to taste

Steps

1. Preheat the air fryer to 375°F/190°C
2. In a large bowl, add all ingredients into a large bowl, mix until all vegetables coated with oil and seasonings.
3. Grease air fryer basket. Place vegetables in a single layer in basket. (you may need to cook in batches.)
4. Air fry for 13 minutes. stirring halfway through cooking time.

Roasted Potatoes

Prep Time
5 Minutes

Cook Time
15 Minutes

Total Time
20 Minutes

Serving Size
4 servings

INGREDIENTS

- 700g baby potatoes, (halved)
- 1/2 tsp garlic powder
- 1/2 tsp onion powder
- Salt & pepper to taste

Steps

1. Preheat air fryer to 400°F/205°C .

2. In a large bowl, add all ingredients. Mix.

3. In a greased air fryer basket, add potatoes in a single layer. (you may need to work in batches).

4. Air Fry for 15 mins, flipping halfway through cooking time.

Garlic Carrots

Prep Time
5 Minutes

Cook Time
15 Minutes

Total Time
20 Minutes

Serving Size
2 servings

INGREDIENTS

- 250g carrots, peeled & cut length-ways
- 2 tsp oil
- 3 garlic cloves, minced
- 1/2 tsp dried thyme
- 1/2 tsp dried oregano
- Salt & pepper to taste

Steps

1. In a bowl, add all ingredients mix until carrots coated with seasoning.

2. Put carrots in a greased air fryer basket.

3. Air fry at 360°F/180°C for 15 minutes, flipping halfway through cooking time.

Courgette Chips

Prep Time
10 Minutes

Cook Time
8 Minutes

Total Time
18 Minutes

Serving Size
4 servings

INGREDIENTS

- 2 courgettes, sliced ¼" thick
- 1 egg
- 2 tbsp milk
- 60g plain flour
- 100g panko bread crumbs
- 100g grated Parmesan cheese
- ½ tsp garlic powder
- ½ tsp Italian seasoning

Steps

1. Prepare three bowls: 1) flour 2) Beaten egg and milk 3) Bread crumbs, cheese, garlic powder and Italian seasoning.
2. Dip each courgette slice into flour, then egg mixture, and then in bread crumb mixture, pressing to coat.
3. Put chips in a greased air fryer basket in a single layer. Air Fry at 400°F/205°C for 8 mins, flipping halfway through cooking time.

Apple Chips

Prep Time
5 Minutes

Cook Time
15 Minutes

Total Time
20 Minutes

Serving Size
4 servings

INGREDIENTS

- 2 apples, cored & sliced into 1/2-cm thick slices
- ¼ tsp cinnamon

Steps

1. Preheat air fryer to 300°F/148°C .
2. In a bowl, add all ingredients mix until apple coated with cinnamon.
3. Add apples in a single layer in air fryer.
4. Air fry for 15 minutes, flipping halfway through cooking time.
5. Transfer to a wire rack and let cool, then serve.

Cauliflower Bites

Prep Time
13 Minutes

Cook Time
7 Minutes

Total Time
20 Minutes

Serving Size
4 servings

INGREDIENTS

- 300g cauliflower florets
- 150g Panko breadcrumbs
- 1 tsp paprika
- 1 tsp garlic powder
- 3 tbsp hot sauce
- 2 tbsp oil
- 2 large eggs, beaten
- Salt & pepper to taste

Steps

1. In a bowl, add cauliflower, oil, hot sauce, garlic powder, paprika, salt, & pepper. Mix until evenly coated.
2. In a small bowl, add eggs. In another small bowl, place breadcrumbs. Dip florets in egg and then coat with breadcrumbs.
3. Transfer cauliflower florets to a greased air fryer basket and spray with cooking spray.
4. Air Fry at 375°F/190°C for 15 mins until golden brown. (flipping halfway through cooking time)

Butternut Squash

Prep Time
5 Minutes

Cook Time
13 Minutes

Total Time
18 Minutes

Serving Size
3 servings

INGREDIENTS

- ½ butternut squash, cut into 1½-cm cubes
- 2 tbsp oil
- 1 tsp Italian seasoning
- 1 tsp garlic powder
- Salt & pepper to taste

Steps

1. In bowl, add all ingredients. Mix to combine.
2. Transfer to a greased air fryer basket in a single layer. (you may need to air fry in batches).
3. Air fry at 400°F/205°C for 13 minutes until tender and crisp. (flipping halfway through cooking time).
4. Serve with crumbled cheese and nuts as a salad or on its own with your favourite sauce or dipping.

Courgette Bites

Prep Time
10 Minutes

Cook Time
15 Minutes

Total Time
25 Minutes

Serving Size
4 servings

INGREDIENTS

- 300g grated courgette
- 100g breadcrumbs
- 50g grated Parmesan cheese
- 1 tablespoon oil
- ½ tsp garlic powder
- ½ tsp paprika
- 1 tsp oregano
- 1 tsp thyme
- 1 large egg
- Salt & pepper to taste

Steps

1. In a bowl, add all ingredients. Mix until combined.
2. Take 2 spoonfuls of the courgette mixture and shape into 3-cm balls. Set aside on a plate.
3. Transfer courgette balls to a greased air fryer basket and spray with cooking spray.
4. Air Fry at 350°F/180°C for 15 mins. (flipping halfway through cooking time).

Jalapeño Poppers

Prep Time
10 Minutes

Cook Time
5 Minutes

Total Time
15 Minutes

Serving Size
12 servings

INGREDIENTS

- 12 jalapeño peppers sliced in halves, deseeded
- 180g cream cheese, softened
- 1 tsp garlic powder
- 120g grated cheddar cheese
- 3 tbsp breadcrumbs
- 1 tbsp butter, melted

Steps

1. Preheat the Air Fryer to 390°F/200°C.
2. In a medium bowl, add cream cheese, garlic powder and cheddae cheese. Mix.
3. In a small bowl, combine breadcrumbs with melted butter.
4. Take each jalapeño half, and fill with cream cheese mixture then top with breadcrumbs.
5. Place in the Air Fryer basket, and air fry for 6 minutes.

Blooming Onion

INGREDIENTS

- 1 yellow onion, peeled
- 240ml buttermilk
- 200g plain flour
- 2 eggs, beaten
- 200g breadcrumbs
- 1 tsp oregano
- 1 tsp onion powder
- 1 tsp smoked paprika
- 1 tsp thyme
- 1 large egg
- Salt & pepper to taste

Steps

1. Cut a small flat spot on the non-root end of the onion. Place the onion root side up. Using a sharp knife starting from the root make a slice downward. Repeat 5 more times. Carefully separate each layer. Soak the onion for 1 hour in buttermilk.
2. Remove onion from butter milk, shake off excess liquid and then coat the onion. Dip in beaten egg, making sure its all covered in egg. Coat with breadcrumbs and seasoning.
3. In a greased air fryer basket, add the onion, spray with cooking spray.
4. Air Fry at 198°C/390°F for 15 mins until golden brown.

Onion Rings

INGREDIENTS

- 2 yellow onion, sliced 1½-cm thick & separated into rings
- 100g plain flour
- 150ml buttermilk
- 1 egg
- 200g panko bread crumbs
- 1/4 tsp paprika
- 1 1/2 tsp mustard powder
- Salt & pepper to taste

Steps

1. Prepare three bowls: 1) flour and seasonings 2) Beaten egg and buttermilk 3) Bread crumbs.
2. Dip each onion ring in buttermilk/egg mixture, then in flour, then the buttermilk/egg mixture again, and finally into breadcrumbs. Brush onion rings with oil.
3. Transfer onion rings into a greased air fryer basket in a single layer (you may need to work in batches).
4. Air fry at 182°C/360°F for 6 minutes . (flipping halfway through cooking time).

Garlic Butter Knots

Prep Time 10 Minutes **Cook Time** 15 Minutes **Total Time** 25 Minutes **Serving Size** 12 servings

INGREDIENTS

Dough
- 1 package active dry yeast
- 1 tsp sugar
- 240ml warm water
- 1/2 tsp salt
- 1 tbsp oil
- 300g plain flour

- 6 tbsp butter, melted
- 1/2 tsp dried oregano
- 1/2 tsp dried parsley
- 1/2 tsp garlic powder
- 1/4 tsp dried basil
- 3 tbsp grated Parmesan Cheese

Steps

1. In small bowl add yeast, sugar and water, mix. Let sit for 10 mins for the yeast to activate.
2. In large bowl add salt, yeast mixture and oil. Add flour gradually and knead until a dough starts to pull from sides of the bowl. Transfer into a floured surface and knead for 3 mins.
3. In a bowl, add melted butter, oregano, parsley, garlic powder, basil, and Parmesan. Mix.
4. Roll out dough into rectangle. Divide into 12 pieces using pizza cutter. Roll each piece into 13-cm rope, 11/2-cm thick. Tie each into a knot. Brush the knots with 1/2 of butter mixture.
5. Transfer knots (in batches) into a greased air fryer basket in a single layer. Air Fry at 180°C/350°F for 15 mins.
6. Remove from air fryer, brush with remaining butter mixture and serve.

Cheesy Pull-Apart Bread

Prep Time 10 Minutes **Cook Time** 4 Minutes **Total Time** 15 Minutes **Serving Size** 8 servings

INGREDIENTS

- 1 white bread loaf
- 8 tablespoons melted butter
- 3 garlic cloves, minced
- 100 grated Mozzarella cheese
- 50g Cheddar cheese

- 2 tbsp chopped fresh parsley
- 1 scallion, finely chopped
- Salt & pepper to taste

Steps

1. Cut loaf in a 1-inch grid pattern not slicing all way through.
2. In a bowl, add melted butter, garlic, parsley, salt & pepper, mix. Brush all bread loaf including the cracks with butter mixture. Fill the cracks with cheese. Sprinkle with chopped scallions.
3. Transfer bread loaf into a greased air fryer basket.
4. Air fry at 176°C/350°F for 4 minutes until golden and cheese is melted.

English Muffins

Prep Time
40 Minutes

Cook Time
11 Minutes

Total Time
51 Minutes

Serving Size
14 servings

INGREDIENTS

- 320ml lukewarm milk
- 1 sachet dried yeast
- 25g caster sugar
- 450g plain flour
- 1/4 teaspoon salt
- 2 tablespoon butter

Steps

1. In a bowl add all ingredients and knead until a dough starts to form. Knead for 3 more mins until smooth. Cover with clingfilm and set aside in a warm place to rise until doubled in size. Roll out dough on a floured surface into rectangle 2-cm thick. Cut out circles of 8-cm. Cover with towel and leave for 30 mins to rise.
2. Preheat Air Fryer to 190°C/375°C.
3. Transfer muffins (in batches) into a greased air fryer basket in a single layer. Air Fry for 11 mins. (flipping halfway through cooking time).
4. Remove from air fryer, let cool and serve.

Soda Bread

Prep Time
10 Minutes

Cook Time
25 Minutes

Total Time
40 Minutes

Serving Size
8 servings

INGREDIENTS

- 1 egg
- 1 tablespoon milk
- 500g plain flour
- 1 teaspoon bicarbonate of soda
- 75g raisins
- 300ml buttermilk

Steps

1. In a mixing bowl, add flour, bicarbonate of soda, salt, sugar and raisins. mix. Add buttermilk, egg and stir. Bring together with hands then transfer dough to floured surface and form into a round loaf shape. Slash the top with a sharp knife.
2. Grease 15cm round cake tin. Transfer the dough to the tin. Brush loaf top with buttermilk.
3. Air fry at 160°C/320°F for 25 minutes. (flipping halfway through cooking time). Insert a toothpick into the center of the loaf. If it comes out clean, then it's done.

Asparagus Parmesan Chips

Prep Time 5 Minutes Cook Time 8 Minutes Total Time 13 Minutes Serving Size 2 servings

INGREDIENTS

- 20 asparagus
- 1 egg
- 1 teaspoon water
- 100 g breadcrumbs
- ⅛ teaspoon of each garlic powder, onion powder, salt, pepper, paprika
- 50g grated parmesan cheese

Steps

1. In a dish, add an egg and water, then beat. Add the asparagus and stir to coat.
2. In a bowl, add breadcrumbs, parmesan and spices. Add asparagus, and mix until coated.
3. Add asparagus to a greased air fryer basket in a single layer. Spray tops with cooking spray.
4. Air fry at 205°C/400°F for 8 minutes . (flipping halfway through cooking time). Serve with your favorite dipping.

Green Beans

Prep Time 5 Minutes Cook Time 11 Minutes Total Time 17 Minutes Serving Size 6 servings

INGREDIENTS

- 450g fresh green beans
- 2 tsp oil
- 1 tsp lemon juice
- 3 garlic cloves , sliced
- 50g grated parmesan
- Salt & pepper to taste

Steps

1. Preheat Air Fryer to 187°C/370°F.
2. In a bowl, add all ingredients and mix.
3. Arrange green beans in a single layer in air fryer basket. Air Fry for 13 mins, stirring halfway through cooking time.

Courgette Fritters

INGREDIENTS

- 2 medium courgettes, grated
- 1 lemon, juice and zest
- 2 egg, beaten
- 100 g plain flour
- 100g your favourite grated cheese
- 1 tsp dried oregano
- Salt & pepper to taste

Steps

1. Preheat an air fryer to 182°C/360°F.
2. Squeeze out as much water as you can from courgettes. Transfer to a large bowl. Add all remaining ingredients. Mix. Shape the mixture into 12 patties.
3. Transfer patties to a greased air fryer basket and spray with cooking spray.
4. Air Fry for 12 mins until golden brown. (flipping halfway through cooking time)

Hasselback Potatoes

Prep Time 10 Minutes Cook Time 40 Minutes Total Time 50 Minutes Serving Size 4 servings

INGREDIENTS

- 1 kg small Maris Piper potatoes
- Melted butter
- Salt & pepper to taste
- 1 tsp rosemary or oregano (optional)

Steps

1. Preheat an air fryer to 180°C/350°F.
2. Place a potato on a chopping board between 2 wooden spoons handles. Cut slits 1/2-cm apart in potatoes, leaving the bottom intact.
3. Drizzle with oil, season with salt & pepper. Arrange the potatoes in a greased air fryer basket.
4. Air Fry for 30 minutes. Remove the basket and brush each potato with butter, then Air Fry for a further 5 minutes, or until golden, crisp and tender.

Aubergine dip

Prep Time 5 Minutes **Cook Time** 35 Minutes **Total Time** 40 Minutes **Serving Size** 4 servings

INGREDIENTS

- 1 aubergine
- 1 garlic clove, minced
- ½ green chilli, finely chopped
- ½ bunch fresh parsley, leaves only & finely chopped
- 1 tablespoon olive oil
- ½ lemon juice
- ½ teaspoon smoked paprika
- Salt & pepper to taste

Steps

1. Preheat Air Fryer to 160°C/330°C.
2. Pierce the aubergine a couple of times with a fork, then Air fry for 35 mins until softened.
3. Remove from air fryer basket and let cool.
4. Scoop the inside of aubergine, place into a bowl or food processor. Add all remaining ingredients and process/or blend with a hand blender until smooth.
5. Serve with bread.

Kale Crisps

Prep Time 10 Minutes **Cook Time** 10 Minutes **Total Time** 20 Minutes **Serving Size** 4 servings

INGREDIENTS

- 225g kale
- 1 tablespoon olive oil
- Salt & pepper to taste

Steps

1. Spread each leaf on a chopping board. Cut the leaves from spine. Tear leaves into small pieces. Transfer to a bowl. Add oil, salt & pepper. Mix until kale coated with oil and seasoning. Transfer to air fryer basket. (You may need to cook in batches)
2. You can cover the kale with an air fryer rack. This helps to avoid the kale from flying around in the air fryer.
3. Air Fry at 176°C/350°F for 4 mins.

Haggis Croquettes

Prep Time 5 Minutes **Cook Time** 20 Minutes **Total Time** 25 Minutes **Serving Size** 4 servings

INGREDIENTS

- 450g hot mashed potatoes
- 100g grated Cheddar cheese
- 4 tablespoons plain flour
- 1 large egg
- 100g cooked haggis

Coating:
- 1 egg
- 2 tbsp milk
- 60g plain flour
- 100g breadcrumbs

Steps

1. In a bowl, add all ingredients and mix until combined. Roll mixture into 20 finger-shaped croquettes.
2. Prepare three bowls: 1) flour 2) Beaten egg and milk 3) Bread crumbs and seasoning.
3. Preheat Air Fryer to 195ºC/385ºC.
4. Dip each croquette into flour, then egg mixture, and then in breadcrumb.
5. Put croquettes in a greased air fryer basket in a single layer. Air Fry for 18 mins, flipping halfway through cooking time.
6. Remove from air fryer, serve.

Garlic Mushrooms

Prep Time 8 Minutes **Cook Time** 12 Minutes **Total Time** 20 Minutes **Serving Size** 2 servings

INGREDIENTS

- 225g mushrooms, halved
- 2 tbsp oil
- 1/2 tsp garlic powder
- 1 tsp. Worcestershire sauce
- 1 lemon juice
- Salt & pepper to taste

Steps

1. In a mixing bowl, add mushrooms,oil, garlic powder, Worcestershire sauce, season with salt & pepper. Mix until combined.
2. Air fry at 380ºF/195ºC for 12 mins, stirring half way through cooking time.
3. Remove from air fryer, add lemon juice and mix. Serve.

Cheesy Stuffed Mushroom

Prep Time 10 Minutes   Cook Time 10 Minutes   Total Time 20 Minutes   Serving Size 8 servings

INGREDIENTS

- 230g button mushrooms
- 120g softened cream cheese
- 1/2 tsp garlic powder
- 1/4 tsp paprika
- 1/4 tsp chili powder
- 50g grated cheese
- Salt & pepper to taste

Steps

1. Remove mushroom stems, dice the stems and set aside.
2. In a bowl, add cream cheese, garlic powder, paprika, chili powder, season with salt & pepper. Mix until smooth. Add in the reserved diced mushroom stems.
3. Spray mushroom tops with cooking spray. Fill mushroom with cream cheese mixture.
4. Put mushrooms in the air fryer basket in a single layer (cook in batches).
5. Air fry at 360°F/180°C for 8 minutes.
6. Top with grated cheese, air fry for another 2 minutes until the cheese is melted.
7. Serve warm or at room temperature.

Crispy Tofu Bites

Prep Time 5 Minutes   Cook Time 35 Minutes   Total Time 40 Minutes   Serving Size 6 servings

INGREDIENTS

- 400g firm/extra firm tofu , (drained)
- 1/2 tsp. lemon zest
- 1/2 tsp. garlic powder
- Salt & pepper to taste

Steps

1. Preheat air fryer at 400°F/205°C . Spray air fryer basket with cooking spray.
2. Squeeze the excess water from tofu . Cut tofu into 2cm thick slices.
3. In bowl, add tofu cubes and spray cooking spray. Sprinkle half of spices. Stir .
4. Put tofu in air fryer basket in a single layer, (you may need to work in batches).
5. Air fry for 30 minutes until golden brown, flipping half way through cooking time.

Yorkshire Pudding

Prep Time
10 Minutes

Cook Time
11 Minutes

Total Time
21 Minutes

Serving Size
12 servings

INGREDIENTS

- 240g plain flour
- 480ml milk
- 4 large eggs
- 1 tsp salt

Steps

1. In a bowl, add flour and salt. Mix, then make a well in the center. Add eggs and milk. Mix until smooth.
2. Grease 12 (180m) Ramekins. Fill ramekins 1/2 way, and place them into the air fryer basket (in batches).
3. Air fry at 380°F/190°C for 11 minutes.
4. Serve warm.

Minced Beef Wellington

Prep Time 30 Minutes   Cook Time 20 Minutes   Total Time 50 Minutes   Serving Size 2 servings

INGREDIENTS

- 1 tbsp butter
- 3 button mushrooms, chopped
- 2 tsp plain flour
- 120g double cream
- 1 large egg yolk
- 1 small onion, finely chopped
- salt & pepper to taste
- 220g minced beef
- 120g refrigerated crescent rolls
- 1 egg, beaten

Steps

1. Preheat air fryer to 300°F/150°C. Grease a baking sheet that will fit in your air fryer.
2. In a saucepan over medium/high heat, add butter & mushrooms, cook for 6 mins. Add flour & pepper stir until combined. Add cream, stir. Bring to a boil, and stir until thickened. Remove from heat and set aside.
3. In a bowl, add egg yolk, onion, 2 tbsp mushroom sauce, salt and pepper. Add minced beef over mixture and mix. Shape into 2 loaves. Unroll crescent dough and separate into 2 rectangles. Place meat loaf on each rectangle. Pinch edges together to seal. brush with egg.
4. Add Wellington in a single layer on baking sheet in air fryer basket. Air fry for 22 mins.
5. Serve Wellingtons with mushroom sauce..

Hash Browns Bake

Prep Time 15 Minutes   Cook Time 30 Minutes   Total Time 30 Minutes   Serving Size 4 servings

INGREDIENTS

- 400g minced beef or turkey
- 1 small onion, chopped
- Salt & pepper to taste
- 480g frozen mini hash browns
- 120ml chicken stock
- 3 tbsp plain flour
- 2 tbsp melted butter
- 120ml milk
- 70g grated cheddar cheese

Steps

1. Preheat air fryer to 350°F/180°C. Grease baking dish that will fit in the air fryer basket.
2. In a large frying pan over medium heat, brown beef and onion, drain. Season with salt & pepper.
3. Transfer to beef to prepared baking dish, top with hash browns. In a bowl, add stock, milk, butter and flour, mix & pour over hash browns. Sprinkle with cheese.
4. Place baking dish in air fryer basket. Air fry for 30 minutes.

Kofta Kebabs

Prep Time 15 Minutes | Cook Time 12 Minutes | Total Time 27 Minutes | Serving Size 4 servings

INGREDIENTS

- 450g minced beef
- 450g minced lamb
- 1 small onion, finely chopped
- 2 garlic cloves, minced
- Handful fresh parsley, chopped
- 2 tsp ground cumin
- Salt & pepper to taste
- 1 tsp allspice
- ½ tsp nutmeg
- ½ tsp paprika
- ¼ tsp cinnamon

Steps

1. In your processor add all ingredients and pulse until smooth.
2. Divide the meat mixture into even into 15 balls. With damp hands, shape the meat to form log-shaped kebabs each about 10cm long. Make sure meat is spread to an even thickness.
3. Add kofta kebabs to the air fryer basket. (You may need to cook in batches).
4. Air fry at 380°F/195°C for 12 mins, flipping halfway through cooking time.

Cheesy Stuffed Meatballs

Prep Time 10 Minutes | Cook Time 10 Minutes | Total Time 20 Minutes | Serving Size 6 servings

INGREDIENTS

- 450g minced beef
- 1 egg
- 30g bread crumbs
- 30g grated parmesan cheese
- 2 cloves garlic, minced
- 1 tsp Italian seasoning
- 1 tsp paprika
- Salt & pepper to taste
- 25g chopped parsley
- 3 tbs milk
- 100g mozzarella cheese, cut into 18 cubes

Steps

1. In a large bowl, add all ingredients except (mozzarella), and mix until combined.
2. Divide meat mixture into 18 balls and place in a baking sheet. Flatten the meatball and place cheese cube in the middle and shape it into a ball covering the cheese.
3. Preheat Air fryer 370°F/190°C. Spray Air fryer basket with cooking spray and add the meatballs on it in a single layer.
4. Air fry for 12 mins until browned, flipping halfway through cooking times. (You may need to work in batches).
5. Once all cooked, serve or you can put into warm marinara sauce.

Steak Bites

Prep Time 7 Minutes Cook Time 8 Minutes Total Time 15 Minutes Serving Size 4 servings

INGREDIENTS

- 1 kg rump steak, (cut into 5cm pieces)
- 2 tbsp oil
- 1 tsp. garlic powder
- 2 tbsp. Worcestershire Sauce
- Salt & pepper to taste

Steps

1. In a mixing bowl, add all ingredients. Mix. Cover and refrigerate for at least 30 minutes.
2. Preheat air fryer to 205°C/400°F for 5 minutes.
3. Spray air fryer basket with cooking spray. Add steak pieces into the basket.
4. Air fry for 6 mins, flipping halfway through cooking times.
5. Remove from air fryer, serve.

Sausage Balls

Prep Time 10 Minutes Cook Time 8 Minutes Total Time 18 Minutes Serving Size 5 servings

INGREDIENTS

- 450g breakfast sausage
- 240g pancake mix
- 1 tsp garlic powder
- 60ml milk
- 80g grated Cheddar Cheese

Steps

1. In a large bowl, add all ingredients. Mix until combined.
2. Using a cookie scoop, scoop the dough into balls.
3. Spray air fryer basket with cooking spray, then place balls in the greased basket with enough space to cook evenly. (You may need to work in batches).
4. Cook at 360°F/182°C 10 minutes.
5. remove and place on a cooling rack and repeat for remaining batches.

Rosemary Garlic Lamp Chops

Prep Time 5 Minutes | **Cook Time** 15 Minutes | **Total Time** 20 Minutes | **Serving Size** 2 servings

INGREDIENTS

- 600g lamb chops , about 7-8 chops
- 3 tbsp oil
- 2 tbsp chopped rosemary
- 1 tsp garlic powder
- Salt & pepper to taste

Steps

1. Pat dry the lamb chops.
2. In a large bowl, add all ingredients and mix to coat lamp chops with seasoning. Cover and refrigerate for 1 hour.
3. Preheat the air fryer at 380°F/195°C for 4 minutes. Spray air fryer basket with cooking spray and put lamb chops in a single layer.
4. Air fry for 15 minutes, flipping halfway through cooking time.

Garlic Butter Steak

Prep Time 12 Minutes | **Cook Time** 18 Minutes | **Total Time** 30 Minutes | **Serving Size** 2 servings

INGREDIENTS

- 2 (170g each) steaks, (2cm thick, rinsed & patted dry)
- 1 tsp. oil
- ½ tsp. garlic powder
- Butter
- Salt & pepper to taste

Steps

1. Preheat the Air Fryer at 400°F/205°C for 5 minutes.
2. Coat steaks with oil. Season both sides with garlic powder, salt & pepper.
3. Spray air fryer basket with cooking spray. Add steaks in air fryer basket in a single layer.
4. Air Fr for 18 mins, flipping halfway through cooking time.
5. Remove from air fryer, add some butter on top of the steak, cover with foil and allow to rest for 4 mins. Serve immediately.

Lasagna

Prep Time
20 Minutes
Cook Time
30 Minutes
Total Time
50 Minutes
Serving Size
12 servings

INGREDIENTS

- 6 Lasagna Sheets
- 450g minced beef or turkey
- 1 tsp Italian seasoning
- 450g cottage cheese
- 225g cream cheese, softened
- 680g jar red pasta sauce
- 170g shredded cheese

Steps

1. Place lasagna sheets into a large dish with water and soak until soft.
2. Preheat air fryer to 350°F/175°C.
3. In a frying pan over medium/high heat brown minced beef & onion. Stir in Italian seasoning. Set aside. Add in cottage and cream cheese to beef and stir.
4. Drain water from lasagna sheets. Layer 20x20 cm pans with half of the lasagna sheets, beef/cheese mixture, and pasta sauce. Repeat. Add grated cheese on top.
5. Air fry uncovered for 30 mins.

Swedish Meatballs

Prep Time
20 Minutes
Cook Time
12 Minutes
Total Time
32 Minutes
Serving Size
4 servings

INGREDIENTS

- 450g minced beef, lean
- 40g bread crumbs
- 1 tbsp parsley
- ¼ tsp ground nutmeg
- ¼ tsp garlic powder
- ¼ tsp allspice
- 25g diced onions
- Salt & pepper to taste
- 1 egg

Steps

1. in a large mixing bowl, add all ingredients. Mix until combined.
2. Using a cookie scoop, scoop into meatballs, and place them into air fryer basket. Cook at 380°F/195°C for 12 mins, flipping halfway through cooking time.

Beef Liver And Onions

Prep Time 5 Minutes **Cook Time** 12 Minutes **Total Time** 17 Minutes **Serving Size** 4 servings

INGREDIENTS

- 450g beef liver, sliced
- 1 large onion, sliced
- Salt & pepper to taste

Steps

1. Season liver and onion with salt and pepper.
2. Spray the air fryer basket with cooking spray. Add liver and onion to the basket.
3. Air fry at 205°C/400°F for 12 mins, mixing halfway through cooking time.

Steak Fajitas

Prep Time 35 Minutes **Cook Time** 10 Minutes **Total Time** 45 Minutes **Serving Size** 6 servings

INGREDIENTS

- 1 ½ kg rump or bavette steak, sliced
- 2 Tablespoon lime juice
- 1 Tablespoon oil
- 1 Tablespoon soy sauce
- 1 garlic clove, minced
- 1 teaspoon cumin
- ½ teaspoon smoked paprika
- 1 green bell pepper, sliced
- 1 yellow bell pepper sliced
- 1 red bell pepper sliced
- 1 onion. sliced
- Salt & pepper to taste

Steps

1. In a small bowl, add sliced steak, lemon juice, oil, soy sauce, garlic, cumin, paprika, salt & pepper. Mix and let set in refrigerator for 30 mins.
2. Remove from refrigerator, drain steak and discard marinade, add peppers and onions to the steak and mix.
3. Line Air fryer basket with foil and coat with cooking spray. Add steak, peppers and onion to the basket.
4. Air at 198°C/390°F for 10 mins, mixing halfway through cooking time.

BBQ Baby Back Ribs

Prep Time 5 Minutes **Cook Time** 35 Minutes **Total Time** 40 Minutes **Serving Size** 4 servings

INGREDIENTS

- 1 ½ kg baby back pork ribs
- 1 tbsp brown sugar
- 1 tbsp white sugar
- 2 tsp smoked paprika
- 1 tsp garlic powder
- ½ tsp ground black pepper
- ½ tsp ground cumin
- ½ tsp onion powder
- 80ml barbeque sauce

Steps

1. Preheat air fryer to 175°C/350°F.
2. Remove membrane from the ribs. Cut ribs into 4 portions.
3. In a small bowl, add all seasonings. Rub seasonings mixture all over ribs. Place ribs in air fryer basket.
4. Air fry ribs for 33 mins, flipping halfway through cooking time. Brush with barbeque sauce, then Air fry for another 5 minutes.

Sausage, Peppers & Onions

Prep Time 10 Minutes **Cook Time** 20 Minutes **Total Time** 30 Minutes **Serving Size** 4 servings

INGREDIENTS

- 5 sausages
- 2 onions, sliced
- 2 green peppers, sliced
- 2 red peppers, sliced
- 2 yellow peppers, sliced
- 3 tbsp oil

Steps

1. Add all ingredients into a large bowl, add oil. Mix to coat in oil.
2. Add sausage to greased air fryer basket and air fry at 198°C/390°F for 20 mins.
3. Add peppers and onions. Air fry at 198°C/390°F for more 7 mins. Mixing halfway through cooking time.
4. Serve.

Standing Rib Roast

Prep Time
5 Minutes

Cook Time
1H15 Mins

Total Time
1H40 Mins

Serving Size
4 servings

INGREDIENTS

- 2 ½ kg standing rib roast/prime rib
- 3 tbsp olive oil
- Salt & pepper to taste
- 1 tsp smoked paprika
- 1 tsp garlic powder
- 10 garlic cloves, minced
- ½ tsp dried rosemary
- ½ tsp dried thyme

Steps

1. Preheat air fryer to 198°C/390°F.
2. Rub the standing rib roast with oil, then sprinkle with salt & pepper, paprika, and garlic powder.
3. Cover the standing rib roast with minced garlic, rosemary and thyme.
4. Place the standing rib roast in greased air fryer basket and Air fry for 20 mins.
5. Reduce heat to 157°C/315°F and continue to Air fry for more 55 mins for medium-rare.
6. Let the standing rib roast rest for 30 mins, then slice and serve.

LONDON BROIL

Prep Time
5 Minutes

Cook Time
8 Minutes

Total Time
23 Minutes

Serving Size
4 servings

INGREDIENTS

- 700g round London Broil
- 4 tbsp oil
- 60ml Worcestershire sauce
- 60ml soy sauce
- 1 garlic clove, minced
- 2 tbsp Italian seasoning
- Salt & pepper to taste

Steps

1. In a large ziplock bag add all ingredients and let marinade for at least 1 hour.
2. Remove the steak from marinade and put in a greased air fryer basket.
3. Air fry for 10 mins at 205°C/400°F (this timing is for medium-rare) increase cooking time until desired preference.
4. Remove London broil from air fryer, let rest for 10 mins before slicing and serving.

Mongolian Beef

Prep Time
30 Minutes

Cook Time
10 Minutes

Total Time
40 Minutes

Serving Size
4 servings

INGREDIENTS

- 450g Flank/Bavette or Ramp Steak, thinly sliced
- 40g cornflour
- 2 tsp oil
- 1/2 tsp ground ginger
- 1 garlic clove, minced
- 120ml soy sauce
- 120ml water
- 150g brown sugar

Steps

1. Coat steak slices with cornflour. Add steak slices to a greased air fryer basket. Air fry for 10 mins at 198°C/390°F. Flipping halfway through cooking time.
2. In a saucepan on medium high heat, add ginger, garlic, oil, soy sauce, water and brown sugar. Stir until combined. Bring to a gentle boil, then remove from heat.
3. Add cooked steak slices in a bowl, pour over the sauce and let set for 5 mins.

Scotch Egg

Prep Time
25 Minutes

Cook Time
10 Minutes

Total Time
35 Minutes

Serving Size
4 servings

INGREDIENTS

- 500g minced beef, (lean)
- 5 eggs
- 1 tsp. dried sage
- ½ tsp red chili flake
- ½ tsp garlic powder
- ½ tsp onion powder
- 60g plain flour
- 2 tbsp milk
- 60g bread crumbs
- Salt & pepper to taste

Steps

1. In saucepan over high heat. bring 1 liter water to a boil; add 4 eggs, boil 5 minutes. Then transfer eggs into bowl full with ice water. Peel the eggs.
2. In a bowl, add minced beef, all spices and season with salt & pepper. Mix until combined.
3. Divide minced beef into 4 portions and form into disks. Place 1 egg in the middle of each disk. Wrap beef around each egg to fully cover egg with beef.
4. Prepare three bowls: 1) flour, 2) egg whisked with milk, and 3) bread crumbs. Dredge each egg in flour, dip in egg then roll in bread crumbs. Refrigerate Scotch egg for 20 minutes.
5. Spray each Scotch egg with cooking spray and place in air fryer. Air fry for 8 mins at 390°F/200°C, flip and air fry for more 7 mins.

Toad in the Hole

Prep Time
10 Minutes

Cook Time
30 Minutes

Total Time
40 Minutes

Serving Size
4 servings

INGREDIENTS

- 450g sausages

Batter:
- 180g plain flour
- 340ml milk
- 2 tbsp butter
- 3 eggs
- ¼ tsp baking powder
- Pinch salt

Steps

1. In a bowl, add all batter ingredients. Whisk until combined and smooth.
2. Grease a baking dish that will fit in your air fryer. Put sausages in the dish, and pour the batter over sausages.
3. Place the dish in the air fryer basket.
4. Air Fry at 190°C/375°F for 30 minutes until cooked through and golden brown. Serve.

Sausage Rolls

Prep Time
15 Minutes

Cook Time
25 Minutes

Total Time
40 Minutes

Serving Size
4 servings

INGREDIENTS

- 2 tbsp oil
- 1 onion, finely chopped
- 6 higher-welfare sausages
- 4 tbsp breadcrumbs
- 250g puff pastry
- 1 egg mixed with 4 tbsp milk

Steps

1. Cut skin of sausages and take meat out. Add it in bowl with onion and breadcrumbs. Then mix until combined.
2. Roll pastry out into a big rectangle on a floured surface and cut it lengthways to 2 long rectangles. Roll the meat into sausage shapes and lay it in the center of each rectangle.
3. Brush pastry with egg/water mixture, then fold one side of the pastry over, wrapping the filling inside. Press down with edge of a spoon to seal. Cut into pieces and brush with egg wash.
4. Spray Air fryer casket with cooking spray. Add sausage rolls on basket in a single layer.
5. Air fry at 165°C/325°F for 25 minutes.

Meatloaf

Prep Time 15 Minutes | **Cook Time** 30 Minutes | **Total Time** 45 Minutes | **Serving Size** 4 servings

INGREDIENTS

- 225g lean minced beef
- 1 egg
- 60ml milk
- 30g breadcrumbs
- 1 small onion, finely chopped
- Salt & pepper to taste
- 60ml ketchup
- 2 tablespoons brown sugar
- 1/4 tsp Worcestershire sauce

Steps

1. In a bowl, add minced beef, egg, milk, breadcrumbs, onion, salt & pepper. Mix until combined.
2. Shape mixture into 2 loaves, place in a greased air fryer basket.
3. Air Fry at 162°C/325°F for 20 mins.
4. In a bowl, add ketchup, brown sugar and Worcestershire sauce, mix until combined. Spoon over meat loaves. Air Fry for more 13 mins.

Stuffed Courgettes

Prep Time 20 Minutes | **Cook Time** 13 Minutes | **Total Time** 33 Minutes | **Serving Size** 4 servings

INGREDIENTS

- 2 large courgettes
- 450g minced beef
- 1 garlic clove, minced
- 200g grated cheese
- 10 cherry tomatoes, quartered
- Salt & pepper to taste

Steps

1. Cut each courgette in half lengthwise, cut a thin slice from bottoms. Scoop out pulp, leaving some shells.
2. In a large frying pan over medium heat, brown beef and garlic. Stir in cheese, tomatoes, season with salt & pepper.
3. Preheat air fryer at 176°C/350°F.
4. Fill each courgette half with beef mixture. Place in greased air fryer basket.
5. Air Fry for 13 mins until tender and cheese is melted.

Roast Lamb with Mint Sauce

Prep Time 4 Minutes   **Cook Time** 6 Minutes   **Total Time** 10 Minutes   **Serving Size** 4 servings

INGREDIENTS

Lamb
- 1.4 kg boneless lamb leg
- 3 garlic cloves, sliced
- 2 tbsp oil
- Salt & pepper to taste

Mint Sauce
- 30g mint leaves, finely chopped
- 2 tbsp brown sugar
- 2 ½ tbsp vinegar
- 2 tbsp boiling water
- 1 tsp salt

Steps

1. With a sharp knife cut 2-cm long slits into the lamb skin. Insert one garlic piece into each slit. Coat the lamb with oil and season with salt & pepper.
2. Preheat air fryer to 180°C/355°F for 2 mins. Add lamb into the basket. Air Fry for 20 mins.
3. In small bowl, add water, mint leaves, vinegar, sugar and salt, stir set aside.
4. After 20 mins. remove lamb from air fryer basket, and rub the mint sauce over the entire lamb. Air Fry for more 20 mins. Repeat process 1 more time and cook for a last 20 mins.
5. Remove from air fryer, wrap lamb leg in tin foil and let rest for 10 mins. Slice and serve.

Baked Chicken Breast

Prep Time 6 Minutes
Cook Time 20 Minutes
Total Time 26 Minutes
Serving Size 3 servings

INGREDIENTS

- 3 (200g each) boneless chicken breast
- 2 tbsp lemon juice
- 1 tbsp oil
- ½ tsp cumin
- ¼ tsp garlic powder
- Salt & pepper to taste

Steps

1. Preheat the Air fryer to 380°F/193°C.
2. In a bowl, add all ingredients. Mix until all chicken coated with seasoning.
3. Add chicken in a greased air fryer basket in a single layer.
4. Air fry for 20 minutes. Flipping halfway through cooking time.
5. Remove from the air fryer and let rest for 5 minutes. Serve.

Herby Chicken Breast

Prep Time 5 Minutes
Cook Time 18 Minutes
Total Time 23 Minutes
Serving Size 2 servings

INGREDIENTS

- 2 (230g each) boneless & skinless chicken breasts
- 2 garlic cloves, minced
- 1/2 tsp. dried basil
- 1/2 tsp. dried rosemary
- 1/2 tsp. paprika
- Salt & pepper to taste

Steps

1. Coat chicken breasts with oil, then season with garlic, paprika, basil, rosemary, salt, & pepper.
2. Spray air fryer basket with cooking spray. Put the chicken in air fryer basket in a single layer.
3. Air Fry at 380°F/193°C for 18 mins, (flipping halfway through cooking time).
4. Let chicken rest for 5 mins. Slice and serve with salad or rice.

BBQ Chicken Wings

Prep Time
10 *Minutes*

Cook Time
10 *Minutes*

Total Time
10 *Minutes*

Serving Size
8 *servings*

INGREDIENTS

- 450g chicken wings
- 1 tbsp oil
- 1 tsp garlic powder
- 1 tsp onion powder
- 2 tbsp Scallions for garnish
- 125ml BBQ sauce
- Salt & pepper to taste

Steps

1. Cut wings into sections (drumettes, wingettes and tips). Discard the tips.
2. In a large bowl, add chicken, oil, add salt, pepper, garlic and onion powder. Mix.
3. Add wings into air fryer basket. Air Fry at 205°C/400°F for 20 mins. (flipping halfway through cooking time).
4. Remove from air fryer into a bowl, add bbq sauce and mix until all coated in sauce.
5. Add wings back in the air fryer at 205°C/400°F for 2 mins.
6. Serve.

BBQ Chicken Legs

Prep Time
5 *Minutes*

Cook Time
15 *Minutes*

Total Time
20 *Minutes*

Serving Size
4 *servings*

INGREDIENTS

- 8 chicken legs
- 2 tsp smoked paprika
- 125ml BBQ saucce
- 1 tsp onion powder
- Salt & pepper to taste

Steps

1. Preheat air fryer at 205°C/400°F.
2. Season chicken legs with salt, pepper and paprika.
3. Add chicken legs to the air fryer basket in a single layer (you may need to work in batches). Air Fry for 20 mins. (Flipping halfway through cooking time).
4. Brush each chicken leg with BBQ sauce. Air Fry for more 2 mins.

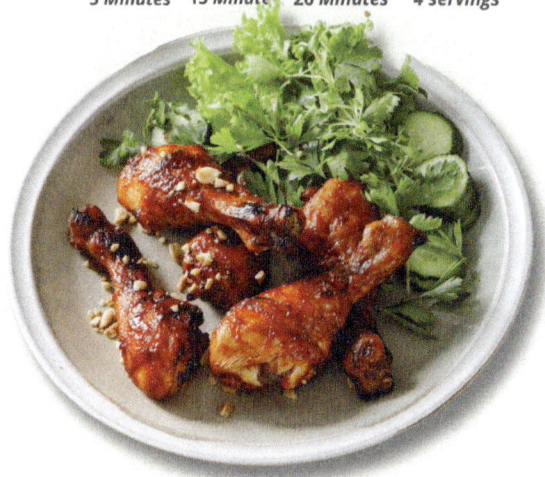

Chicken Kabobs

Prep Time 10 Minutes Cook Time 15 Minutes Total Time 2h 10Minutes Serving Size 4 servings

INGREDIENTS

- 900g skinless chicken thighs/breasts, cut into bite-size cubes
- 120ml soy sauce
- 60ml milk
- 3 tbsp lemon juice
- 3 tbsp golden syrup
- 1 tbsp Thai red curry paste

Steps

1. In a bowl, add soy sauce, milk, lemon juice, golden syrup, and curry paste. Mix, add chicken and let marinate for 1 hour.
2. Soak bamboo skewers in water for 30 mins.
3. Thread marinated chicken onto skewers.
4. Air Fry at 175°C/350°F for 15 mins, (Flipping halfway through cooking time).

Chicken Quesadilla

Prep Time 3 Minutes Cook Time 7 Minutes Total Time 10 Minutes Serving Size 2 servings

INGREDIENTS

- 2 corn tortillas
- 3 tbsp guacamole
- 60g grated cheddar cheese
- 100g cooked chicken breast cubes

Steps

1. Preheat air fryer to 170°C/325°F.
2. Spray air fryer basket with cooking spray, add the first tortilla inside basket. Spread on guacamole, add cheese and chicken and then top with second tortilla. Use a toothpick to secure the top tortilla in place.
3. Air Fry for 7 mins, (Flipping halfway through cooking time).
4. Cut & serve.

Chicken Burgers

Prep Time 5 Minutes **Cook Time** 15 Minutes **Total Time** 20 Minutes **Serving Size** 4 servings

INGREDIENTS

- 450g minced chicken
- 3 garlic cloves, minced
- 1 tbsp Worchestershire sauce
- salt & pepper to taste

Steps

1. In a bowl add all ingredients. Shape into four patties.
2. Add two patties to a greased air fryer basket.
3. Air Fry at 182°C/360°F for 12 minutes. (Flipping halfway through cooking time).

Chicken Parmesan

Prep Time 12 Minutes **Cook Time** 13 Minutes **Total Time** 25 Minutes **Serving Size** 4 servings

INGREDIENTS

- 700g boneless skinless chicken breasts, cut in half lengthway
- 2 eggs
- 80g breadcrumbs
- 25g grated Parmesan cheese
- 500ml marinara sauce
- 120g grated mozzarella cheese
- Salt & pepper to taste

Steps

1. Pound chicken breasts into thinner pieces. Season with salt & pepper.
2. In a bowl, add breadcrumbs and Parmesan cheese. Mix. In another bowl, whisk eggs and set aside.
3. Dip each piece of chicken in egg and then dredge it in the breadcrumb mixture. Spray both sides of chicken with cooking spray.
4. Put chicken in single layer in air fryer basket. Air Fry at 185°C/365°F for 8 mins. Flip and top chicken with marinara sauce and mozzarella cheese.
5. Air fry for another 3 mins.

Garlic Parmesan Chicken Bites

Prep Time 10 Minutes Cook Time 15 Minutes Total Time 20 Minutes Serving Size 4 servings

INGREDIENTS

- 700g boneless skinless chicken breasts, (cut into about 2.5cm chunks)
- 2 tbsp oil
- 2 tsp Worcestershire sauce
- 1/2 tsp dried basil
- 1 tsp garlic powder
- 1 tsp onion powder
- 2 tbsp plain flour
- 3 tbsp grated Parmesan cheese
- Salt & pepper to taste

Steps

1. In a large bowl, add all ingredients (except Parmesan). Mix.
2. Spray air fryer basket with cooking spray. Add chicken into the basket in a single layer.
3. Air Fry at 180°C/360°F for 18 mins. (Flipping halfway through cooking time).
4. Add Parmesan cheese, Air Fry for another minute. Serve warm.

Turkey Meatballs

Prep Time 10 Minutes Cook Time 10 Minutes Total Time 20 Minutes Serving Size 4 servings

INGREDIENTS

- 700g minced turkey/chicken
- 1 red bell pepper, (finely chopped)
- 30g parsley, (finely chopped)
- 1 egg
- 1 tbsp. Italian seasoning
- Salt & pepper to taste

Steps

1. Preheat the Air Fryer to 205°C/400°F.
2. In a bowl, add all ingredients. Mix.
3. Shape mixture into 3-cm meatballs.
4. Add meatballs in a greased air fryer basket in a single layer (you may need to work in batches). Air fry for 10 minus.
5. Serve.

Tandoori Chicken

Prep Time 4 Minutes   Cook Time 6 Minutes   Total Time 10 Minutes   Serving Size 4 servings

INGREDIENTS

- 700g boneless chicken thighs, cut into chunks
- 250g yogurt
- 2 tsp grated fresh ginger
- 1 tsp cumin
- 1 tsp chilli powder
- 1 tsp lemon juice
- 3 tsp garam masala
- 2 garlic cloves, minced
- 1 tsp oil
- 2 drops red gel food coloring
- Salt & pepper to taste

Steps

1. In a bowl, add all ingredients and mix together until chicken coated in the marinade. cover and refrigerate for at least 1 hour.
2. Preheat the air fryer to 205°C/400°F, then grease the basket and the chicken.
3. Air Fry for 15 mins (Flipping halfway through cooking time).
4. Serve.

Chicken Cordon Bleu

Prep Time 15 Minutes   Cook Time 20 Minutes   Total Time 40 Minutes   Serving Size 2 servings

INGREDIENTS

- 2 boneless, skinless chicken breasts
- 1 tbsp Dijon mustard
- 4 slices cheddar cheese
- 16 slices salami
- 2 toothpicks
- 30g plain flour
- 1 egg, beaten
- 60g panko/bread crumbs
- 40g grated Parmesan cheese

Steps

1. Slice each chicken breast horizontally through middle, do not cut all way through to other side. Open the two sides, spread out like open book. Place between two sheets of cling film, pound the chicken to a 1/2-cm thickness.
2. Season each with salt & pepper. Spread mustard on top. Place 1 cheese slice on each breast. Top each with 8 slices of salami and another cheese slice. Roll up, secure with toothpick.
3. Prepare three bowls: 1) flour, 2) Beaten egg 3) Bread crumbs. Dredge each breast in flour, dip in egg then roll in bread crumbs. Refrigerate for 5 mins.
4. Preheat air fryer at 176°C/350°F. Add chicken in a single layer in a greased air fryer basket.
5. Air Fry for 18 mins. (flipping and spraying with cooking spray halfway through cooking time).

Roasted Whole Chicken

Prep Time 15 Minutes   **Cook Time** 20 Minutes   **Total Time** 35 Minutes   **Serving Size** 6 servings

INGREDIENTS

- 1 ½ kg whole chicken
- 2 tablespoon oil
- 2 tbsp smoked paprika
- 1 tbsp garlic powder
- 1 tbsp dried thyme
- Salt & pepper to taste

Steps

1. Rup chicken with oil, then sprinkle with spices. Make sure to coat chicken all over and inside with spices.
2. Place the chicken breast-side down into greased air fryer basket.
3. Air Fry to 177°C/350°F for 60 mins. (flipping halfway through cooking time).
4. Remove from the air fryer and rest 10 mins before serving.

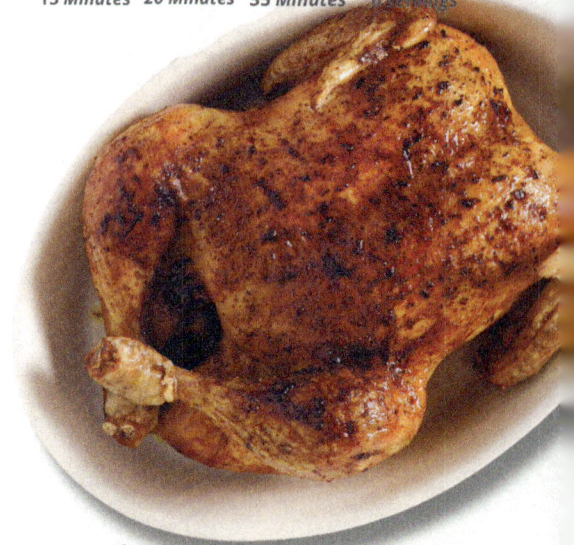

Cornish Game Hens

Prep Time 10 Minutes   **Cook Time** 45 Minutes   **Total Time** 55 Minutes   **Serving Size** 4 servings

INGREDIENTS

- 2 Cornish hens
- 2 tbsp oil
- 1 tsp dried thyme
- 1 tsp dried sage
- ½ tsp smoked paprika
- 1 lemon juice
- 4 garlic cloves, minced
- 1 whole lemon, quartered
- Salt & pepper to taste

Steps

1. In a bowl add all ingredients. Mix until hens coated with marinade.
2. Preheat air fryer to 190°C/375°F.
3. Add 2 lemon quarters and half the garlic in the cavity of each bird.
4. Place hens in a greased air fryer basket or a sheet pan that will fit in your air fryer, Airy Fry for 45 mins. Cooking times will vary depending on the size of your hens.
5. Let rest for 6 mins before serving.

Chicken Shawarma

Prep Time 20 *Minutes* Cook Time 12 *Minutes* Total Time 32 *Minutes* Serving Size 12 *servings*

INGREDIENTS

- 1 kg boneless skinless chicken thighs, sliced

Marinade:
- 4 tbsp oil
- 5 garlic cloves, minced
- 50ml fresh lemon juice

- 2 tsp smoked paprika
- 2 tsp ground cumin
- 1 tsp ground coriander
- ¼ tsp dried chilli flakes
- ¼ tsp turmeric
- Salt & pepper to taste

Steps

1. In a bowl, add marinade ingredients, mix. Place chicken in a ziplock bag and add marinade. Coat chicken with marinade. Place in refrigerator for 30 mins.
2. Add chicken slices to a greased air fryer basket.
3. Air Fry at 195°C/380°F for 10 minutes. (stirring halfway through cooking time).
4. Serve with flat bread, over salad or rice.

Chicken Parmesan

Prep Time 20 *Minutes* Cook Time 12 *Minutes* Total Time 32 *Minutes* Serving Size 12 *servings*

INGREDIENTS

- 2 boneless, skinless chicken breasts, pounded to 1-cm thick
- 3 tbsp oil
- 2 tsp garlic powder
- 300g tomato/marinara sauce
- 2 tsp basil
- 1 ½ tsp oregano

- 50g plain flour
- 1 large egg, beaten
- 100g panko/breadcrumbs
- 80g grated Parmesan cheese
- 4 slices mozzarella cheese
- Salt & pepper to taste

Steps

1. Season chicken with salt & pepper.
2. Prepare three bowls: 1) flour 2) Beaten egg and 3) Panko, parmesan and spices. Dredge each breast in flour, dip in egg then roll in Panko mixture.
3. Air Fry at 205°C/400°F for 10 minutes. (flipping halfway through cooking time).
4. Top with marinara and mozzarella. Air Fry again for 3 mins until cheese is melted.

Crispy Fried Chicken

Prep Time
5 Minutes

Cook Time
8 Minutes

Total Time
13 Minutes

Serving Size
4 servings

INGREDIENTS

- 1 kg chicken legs
- 1 1/2 tsp garlic powder
- 1 1/2 tsp smoked paprika
- 1 tsp onion powder
- 1 tsp dried oregano
- 1 tbsp oil
- 120g self-rising flour
- 50g corflour
- 2 eggs
- 1 tbsp hot sauce
- 2 tbsp milk
- 60ml water
- Salt & pepper to taste

Steps

1. In a bowl, add garlic & onion powder, oregano, paprika, salt and pepper. Mix. Add chicken to the bowl and coat with spice mixture. transfer to a clean plate.
2. In a large plastic bag, add flour, cornstarch, and remaining spice mix.
3. In another bowl, add eggs, hot sauce, milk, and water. Mix.
4. Dredge each chicken leg in flour mixture, shaking off the excess. Let set for 5 mins.
5. Dip chicken in egg then coat with flour mixture. Let chicken set for 15 mins.
6. Spray each chicken leg with cooking spray. Place in a greased air fryer basket in a single layer. (you may need to work in batches)
7. Air Fry at 177°C/350°F for 18 mins. (flipping and spraying with cooking spray halfway through cooking time). Remove and let chicken set for 5 mins. Then serve.

Hunters Chicken

Prep Time
5 Minutes

Cook Time
8 Minutes

Total Time
13 Minutes

Serving Size
4 servings

INGREDIENTS

- 4 chicken breasts
- 8 strips streaky beef bacon
- 240ml BBQ sauce
- 60g grated cheddar cheese
- 60g grated mozzarella cheese
- Salt & pepper to taste

Steps

1. Wrap each chicken breast in two strips of bacon.
2. Transfer chicken to a baking dish that will fit in air fryer. Place dish in air fryer.
3. Air Fry at 190° C/375° F for 25 mins. Remove baking dish from air fryer. Spoon the BBQ sauce on chicken, then sprinkle with cheese. Air Fry for more 5 mins. Serve with mash & vegetables.

54

Potato & Chicken Bake

Prep Time 15 Minutes **Cook Time** 26 Minutes **Total Time** 40 Minutes **Serving Size** 2 servings

INGREDIENTS

- 2 cooked chicken breasts, shredded
- 2 potatoes, peeled & thinly sliced
- 150ml double cream
- 125 g sour cream/cream cheese, softened
- 50g your favourite grated cheese
- 1 tbsp smoked paprika
- Salt & pepper to taste

Steps

1. Boil potatoes in boiling water on high heat until just cooked.
2. Arrange potatoes in baking dish that will fit in your air fryer and top with a layer of shredded chicken. Repeat until all potatoes and chicken are used.
3. In a bowl, add double cream, sour cream/cream cheese, smoked paprika, season with salt & pepper and pour over chicken and potatoes. Top with grated cheese.
4. Air Fry at 177°C/350°F for 26 mins.

Orange Chicken

Prep Time 10 Minutes **Cook Time** 20 Minutes **Total Time** 30 Minutes **Serving Size** 5 servings

INGREDIENTS

- 700g boneless chicken, bite-sized pieces
- 1 egg beaten
- 2 tbsp cornflour
- ½ tsp smoked paprika
- 1 tsp sesame oil
- Salt & pepper to taste

Orange sauce:
- 1 tablespoon Sesame oil

- 1 tsp minced ginger
- 1 garlic cloves, minced
- 2 tsp Soy Sauce
- 2 tsp White Vinegar
- 150 ml orange juice
- 3 tbsp brown sugar
- 1 tbsp cornflour mixed with 2 tbsp water

Steps

1. Preheat air fryer at 205°C/400°F for 5 minutes
2. In a bowl, add chicken pieces, egg and sesame oil. Mix. Add cornflour, paprika, salt & pepper. Mix until chicken coated.
3. Transfer chicken to air fryer basket in single layer (in batches). Air fry for 20 mins, flipping halfway through cooking time.
4. In a frying pan over medium-high heat, add oil and garlic. Sauté for 2 mins. Add soy sauce, vinegar, orange juice and brown sugar. Stir and add cornflour mixture. Stir until slightly thickened. Remove from heat, add air fried chicken. Mix until chicken is coated with sauce.
5. Serve over rice.

Chicken and Veggies

Prep Time 5 Minutes **Cook Time** 15 Minutes **Total Time** 20 Minutes **Serving Size** 4 servings

INGREDIENTS

- 450g chicken breast, chopped into bite-size pieces
- 1 courgette, chopped
- 3 bell pepper chopped (any colors you like)
- 1 onion chopped
- 2 cloved garlic minced
- 1/2 tsp of each (garlic powder, dried oregano, dried rosemary)
- Salt & pepper to taste

Steps

1. Preheat air fryer to 205°C/400°F.
2. In a large mixing bowl, add chicken and vegetables Add the oil and seasoning and mix.
3. Add the chicken and vegetables to the air fryer basket (you may have to cook in batches).
4. Air Fry for 10 minutes , stirring halfway through cooking time.

Chicken Fried Rice

Prep Time 5 Minutes **Cook Time** 20 Minutes **Total Time** 25 Minutes **Serving Size** 4 servings

INGREDIENTS

- 600g cooked white rice, cold
- 150g cooked chicken, diced
- 160g frozen peas and carrots
- 6 tbsp soy sauce
- 1 tbsp oil
- 1 onion, diced

Steps

1. In a bowl, add rice, oil and soy sauce and mix. Add frozen peas & carrots, onion and chicken and mix.
2. Pour the rice mixture into the nonstick pan. Place the pan into the Air Fryer.
3. Air Fry at 182°C/360°F for 20 minutes .
4. Remove the pan from the Air Fryer. Serve.

Prawn Tacos

Prep Time
3 Minutes

Cook Time
7 Minutes

Total Time
10 Minutes

Serving Size
4 servings

INGREDIENTS

- 450g small prawn raw, peeled, deveined, tails-off
- 1 tbsp oil
- ¾ tsp chili powder
- ¾ tsp garlic powder
- ½ tsp cumin
- ½ tsp onion powder
- Salt & pepper to taste
- 4 flour tortillas or corn tortillas
- shredded cabbage
- sliced avocados
- crumbled feta cheese
- lemon wedges

Steps

1. In a bowl, add prawn, oil, and all seasonings. Mix.
2. Place prawn in a greased air fryer basket. Air Fry at 400°F/204°C for 8 minutes.
3. Assemble tortillas with prawn, cabbage, and cheese . Place in air fryer basket and Air Fry at 400°F/204°C for 1 minute.
4. Remove tacos from the air fryer and serve.

Salmon Nuggets

Prep Time
20 Minutes

Cook Time
7 Minutes

Total Time
30 Minutes

Serving Size
4 servings

INGREDIENTS

- 100g breadcrumbs
- 50g grated Parmesan cheese
- 1 large egg
- 450g skinless salmon fillet, cut into 4-cm pieces

Steps

1. Preheat air fryer 200°C/390°F.
2. Prepare two bowls: 1) parmesan and breadcrumbs 2) whisked egg . Dip each scallop in egg then roll in parmesan and breadcrumbs mixture. Place on a plate a spray with cooking spray.
3. Transfer salmon nuggets into a greased air fryer basket and Air fry at 370°F/190°C for 7 minutes. . (flipping and spraying with cooking spray halfway through cooking time).
4. Serve with your favourite sauce.

Breaded Scallops

Prep Time
10 Minutes

Cook Time
4 Minutes

Total Time
15 Minutes

Serving Size
4 servings

INGREDIENTS

- 100g crushed salted buttery crackers
- ½ teaspoon garlic powder
- ½ teaspoon smoked paprika
- 2 tablespoons melted butter, melted
- 450g scallops, patted dry
- Salt & pepper to taste

Steps

1. Preheat air fryer 200°C/390°F.
2. Prepare two bowls: 1) crushed crackers and seasonings 2) Melted butter. Dip each scallop in butter then roll in coconut/crushed crackers mixture.
3. Place in a greased air fryer basket (in batches) in a single layer.
4. Air Fry for 4 minutes. (flipping halfway through cooking time).
5. Remove tacos from the air fryer, add the toppings and serve.

Salmon Bites

Prep Time
5 Minutes

Cook Time
8 Minutes

Total Time
15 Minutes

Serving Size
2 servings

INGREDIENTS

Lemon Sauce
- 150g plain Greek yogurt
- 2 tbsp lemon juice
- ½ tbsp oil
- 2 tbsp fresh dill, chopped
- ½ tbsp English mustard
- ¼ tsp garlic powder

Salmon Bites
- 500g skinless salmon fillets, Cubed
- 1 tsp avocado oil
- ½ tsp garlic powder
- salt and pepper to taste

Steps

1. Place salmon into a bowl. Add oil, garlic powder, salt and pepper. Mix.
2. Place salmon into air fryer basket in a single layer.
3. Air fry at 370°F/190°C for 10 minutes.
4. Combine all the ingredients for the sauce in a bowl.
5. Serve the bites with salad or on its own with sauce.

Crispy Fish Fillets

Prep Time
5 Minutes

Cook Time
15 Minutes

Total Time
20 Minutes

Serving Size
4 servings

INGREDIENTS

- 450g white fish fillets (1.5cm thick)
- 1 egg
- 60g yellow cornmeal
- 1 tsp paprika
- ½ tsp garlic powder
- Salt & pepper to taste

Steps

1. Preheat air fryer 200°C/390°F.
2. Prepare two bowls: 1) cornmeal and seasonings 2) beaten egg. Dip each fish fillet in egg then roll in cornmeal mixture.
3. Place fish into a greased air fryer basket. Spray with cooking spray.
4. Air Fry for 10 minutes, flip halfway through cooking time. If its not fully cooked, return to air fryer and cook 7 minutes.
5. Once done, squeeze with lemon. Serve immediately.

Parmesan Crusted Salmon

Prep Time
5 Minutes

Cook Time
8 Minutes

Total Time
13 Minutes

Serving Size
8 servings

INGREDIENTS

- 2 salmon fillets
- 60g mayonnaise
- 1 tsp of each (garlic powder, onion powder, dried basil, dried oregano and dried thyme)
- shredded parmesan cheese to taste

Steps

1. Preheat the air fryer at 400°F/204°C.
2. In a bowl, mix mayonnaise, and herbs.
3. Place the salmon in a greased air fryer basket.
4. Spread the herb mayonnaise mixture on the top of salmon filets. Top with parmesan cheese.
5. Cook at 350°F/175°C for 8 minutes.

Maple-Dijon Glaze Salmon

Prep Time 4 Minutes Cook Time 15 Minutes Total Time 20 Minutes Serving Size 4 servings

INGREDIENTS

- 1 tbsp oil
- 4 salmon fillets

Maple-Dijon Glaze:
- 3 tbsp butter
- 3 tbsp golden/Mable syrup
- 1 tbsp Dijon mustard
- 1 lemon juiced
- 1 garlic clove, minced
- Salt & pepper to taste

Steps

1. Preheat air fryer 200°C/395°F.
2. Drizzle oil over salmon; season with salt & pepper. Transfer salmons to a greased air fryer basket in single layer. Air Fry for 6 minutes.
3. In a saucepan over medium heat, add all glaze ingredients and stir for 2 minutes until thickens.
4. Drizzle salmon fillets with glaze right before serving.

Coconut Prawns

Prep Time 30 Minutes Cook Time 15 Minutes Total Time 45 Minutes Serving Size 6 servings

INGREDIENTS

- 60g plain flour
- 2 eggs
- 50g unsweetened shredded coconut
- 50g breadcrumbs
- 350g uncooked prawn, peeled and deveined
- Salt & pepper to taste

Steps

1. Preheat air fryer to 200°C/395°F.
2. Prepare three bowls: 1) flour, salt & pepper 2) Beaten egg 3) Coconut & Breadcrumbs. Dredge each prawn in flour, dip in egg then roll in coconut/breadcrumb mixture.
3. Place prawn on a plate. Coat prawn with cooking spray.
4. Place the prawn in air fryer basket in single layer (in batches).
5. Air Fry for 6 minutes. Flipping halfway through cooking time.

Prawn & Vegetables

Prep Time 25 Minutes **Cook Time** 20 Minutes **Total Time** 45 Minutes **Serving Size** 4 servings

INGREDIENTS

- 300g Small prawn Peeled & Deveined
- 1 bag of frozen mixed Vegetables
- 1 Tbsp Cajun Seasoning or your favourite seasoning mix

Steps

1. Add the prawn and vegetables to air fryer.
2. Top it with Cajun seasoning and spray with cooking spray.
3. Air Fry at 355°F/180°C for 10 minutes.
4. Open air fryer and mix prawn and vegetables.
5. Continue cooking for an additional 10 minutes.
6. Serve over rice.

Tilapia

Prep Time 10 Minutes **Cook Time** 12 Minutes **Total Time** 22 Minutes **Serving Size** 4 servings

INGREDIENTS

- 4 tilapia filets
- 1 tsp chili powder
- 1 tsp garlic powder
- Salt & pepper to taste
- 100g breadcrumbs

Steps

1. Spray tilaipa fillets with cooking spray or oil and sprinkle with spices and set aside.
2. Add breadcrumbs in shallow dish. place tilapia into breadcrumbs and gently press breadcrumb mixture into the fish. repeat for each filet.
3. Air Fry fillets at 400°F/205°C for 12 minutes in air fryer basket. Flip fillets halfway through cooking.

Lemon Pepper Prawn

Prep Time 5 Minutes
Cook Time 10 Minutes
Total Time 15 Minutes
Serving Size 2 servings

INGREDIENTS

- 1 lemon, juiced
- ¼ teaspoon paprika
- ¼ teaspoon garlic powder
- 350g uncooked medium prawn, peeled and deveined
- Salt & pepper to taste

Steps

1. Preheat air fryer to 200°C/395°F.
2. In a bowl, add all ingredients and mix.
3. Place prawns in air fryer basket. Air fry for 7 minutes.

Salmon Fajitas

Prep Time 5 Minutes
Cook Time 10 Minutes
Total Time 15 Minutes
Serving Size 4 servings

INGREDIENTS

- 2-4 salmon fillets
- 1 fajita seasoning
- 3 bell peppers sliced
- 1 onion, sliced
- Flour tortillas

Toppings
- 1-2 avocados
- 1-2 limes
- shredded cabbage

Steps

1. Pat the salmon dry with paper towels.
2. Place the salmon on a foil sling and surround it with the peppers and onions in the air fryer basket. Lightly spray with cooking spray and rub salmon with fajita seasoning.
3. Cook at 350°F/175°C for 10 minutes .
4. Remove from air fryer and serve on tortillas with avocado, lime, shredded cabbage.

Fish & Chips

INGREDIENTS

- 900g cod fillets
- 60g flour
- 30g cornstarch
- 1 tbsp sugar
- 120ml cold water
- 1 egg
- 100g plain flour
- 100g breadcrumbs
- Salt & pepper to taste

- For the chips
- 1¼ kg, peeled and cut into 1/2 inch/1.5cm long fries
- Salt & pepper to taste

Steps

1. Soak potatoes in a bowl of cold water for 30 minutes.
2. In a bowl, whisk 60g flour and cornstarch. In another bowl, stir together 100g flour, garlic powder, onion powder, salt, pepper, and baking soda. Pour in cold water and stir to combine. (if too thick add more water)
3. Dredge each fish piece in flour mixture, then in the batter. Place the fish pieces back in the flour mixture to fully coat.
4. Line air fryer basket with parchment paper and spray with cooking spray.add fish into basket. (work in batches) Spray tops of fish with cooking spray. Cook at 400°F/200°C for 5 minutes. Flip and spray with cooking spray. Air fry for 4 minutes,until golden brown.
5. Remove from air fryer to a plate and cover with foil. Set aside.
6. drain potatoes and dry them with a towel. spray air fryer basket with cooking spray. Place and spray with cooking spray. Air fry the potatoes at 400°F/200°C for 7 minutes. Flip, cook for 7 minutes unti golden brown and crispy. Sprinkle with salt and pepper. Serve the fish and chips.

Prawn Boil

INGREDIENTS

- 450g baby potatoes
- 60ml water
- 225g sausage, sliced
- 1 cop corn, cut into 5cm pieces
- 1 onion, sliced
- 4 tablespoons oil
- 450g raw large prawn, peeled and deveined
- 1 tsp chili powder
- 1 tsp garlic powder
- Salt & pepper to taste

Steps

1. Place potatoes in a microwave-safe bowl. Add water and microwave on high for 5 minutes. Cut potatoes in half lengthwise and place in a large bowl along with sausage, corn, 2 tbsp oil, half of seasoning and onion.
2. In another bowl, add prawns add remaining and seasoning; stir to coat.
3. Place potato mixture in air fryer basket and Air Fry at 400°F/205°C for 10 minutes. Stir and Air Fry for another 5 minutes. Add 1/2 of the prawns and Air Fry for 5 more minutes. Transfer to a serving plate and repeat with remaining potato mixture and prawns .

Tuna Burgers

INGREDIENTS

- 1 egg, beaten
- 50g breadcrumbs
- Handful finely chopped celery
- 80ml mayonnaise
- 1 small onion, finely chopped
- 200g tinned light tuna in water
- Salt & pepper to taste

Steps

1. In a large bowl, combine all ingredients. Shape into 4 patties.
2. Spray air fryer basket with non-stick spray and place patties (in basket) in basket.
3. Air Fry at 350°F/177°C for 12 minutes. (Flipping halfway through cooking time).

Salmon and Potatoes Bake

Prep Time
5 Minutes

Cook Time
10 Minutes

Total Time
15 Minutes

Serving Size
4 servings

INGREDIENTS

- 225g red potatoes, cut into bite size pieces
- 4 tbsp oil divided
- 5 tbsp your favorite seasoning mix divided
- 800g salmon fillets
- Salt & pepper to taste

Steps

1. Combine the potatoes in a large bowl with 2½ tbsp oil and 3½ tbsp Seasoning Mix.
2. Place potatoes in air fryer basket and cook at 350°F/176°C for 7 minutes.
3. brush salmon fillets both sides with remaining oil, and season with remaining Seasoning.
4. Stir potatoes . Add salmon on top and cook at 350°F/176°C for 10 minutes.
5. Remove salmon from the air fryer basket. Serve..

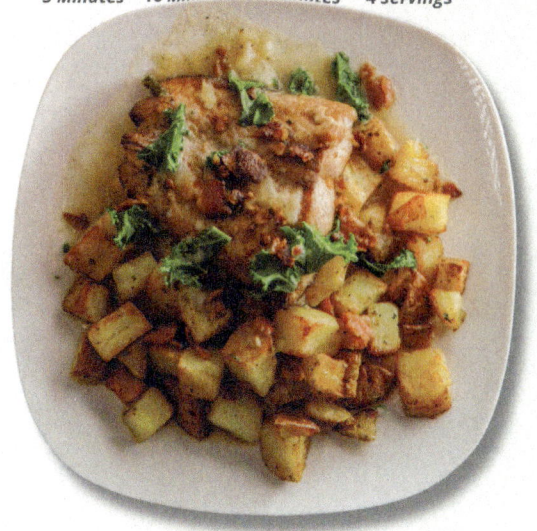

Crab Cakes

Prep Time
10 Minutes

Cook Time
10 Minutes

Total Time
20 Minutes

Serving Size
4 servings

INGREDIENTS

- 450g lump crabmeat
- 60g mayonnaise
- 30g breadcrumbs
- 60g plain flour
- 1 large egg
- 1 scallion sliced
- 1 tbsp Worcestershire sauce
- juice of half lemon
- 1 tbsp Worcestershire sauce
- juice of half lemon
- Salt & pepper to taste

Steps

1. In a large bowl, add all ingredients . Mix and shape into patties.
2. Place in air fryer basket. Cook at 360°F/182°C for 12 minutes until golden brown

Strawberry Rhubarb Crisp

Prep Time 7 Minutes   **Cook Time** 18 Minutes   **Total Time** 25 Minutes   **Serving Size** 5 servings

INGREDIENTS

- 450g strawberries, (hulled & halved)
- 450g rhubarb, trimmed & cut into 1.5cm pieces
- 50g + 3 tbsp sugar, divided
- 1 tbsp cornflour
- 6 tbsp unsalted butter, cut into small cubes
- 100g plain flour
- ¼ tsp salt
- 30g almonds, chopped

Steps

1. Preheat the air fryer to 350°F/175°C. Spray small ramekins with cooking spray and set aside.
2. In a bowl, add strawberries, rhubarb, 50g sugar and cornflour. Mix.
3. In another bowl, add butter and flour, rubbing together with hands until they resemble sand texture. Then, add 3 tbsp sugar, salt & almonds and mix.
4. Divide the fruit mixture among the ramekins and top with the crumble mixture. Put in the air fryer basket and air fry for 18 minutes.

Banana Nut Muffins

Prep Time 10 Minutes   **Cook Time** 14 Minutes   **Total Time** 24 Minutes   **Serving Size** 7 servings

INGREDIENTS

- 3 ripe bananas
- 2 eggs, beaten
- 120g melted butter
- 75g caster sugar
- 50g toasted nuts, finely chopped
- 1 tsp vanilla essence
- 1 tsp baking soda
- ¼ tsp baking powder
- 220g plain flour

Steps

1. Spray silicon muffin liners with cooking spray and set aside
2. Mash Bananas in a bowl, add sugar, butter, eggs, vanilla and mix . Add flour, baking powder nuts and baking soda to the wet ingredients, then mix to combine.
3. Scoop batter into prepared muffin liners. Transfer to the air fryer basket.
4. Air fry at 330°F/166°C for 14 mins until inserted tooth pick comes out clean.

Lemonade Scones

Prep Time 45 Minutes   **Cook Time** 15 Minutes   **Total Time** 60 Minutes   **Serving Size** 16 servings

INGREDIENTS

- 500g self-raising flour
- 70g caster sugar
- 300ml double cream
- 180ml lemonade
- 1 tsp vanilla essence
- Buttermilk, for brushing

Steps

1. In bowl, add flour, sugar, cream, lemonade and vanilla. Gently mix until dough just comes together.
2. Transfer dough onto a floured surface. Knead until just smooth. Press the dough to a 2.5cm thick round. Cut out 16 scones.
3. Spray air fryer basket with cooking spray. Place 5 scones in basket. Brush top with buttermilk. (cook in batches)
4. Air fry at 320°F/160°C for 15 minutes. Serve warm.

Blueberry Scones

Prep Time 10 Minutes   **Cook Time** 6 Minutes   **Total Time** 16 Minutes   **Serving Size** 16 servings

INGREDIENTS

- 180g butter slightly softened
- 250g plain flour
- 50g sugar
- 2 tsp baking powder
- 1 large egg
- 140g fresh or frozen blueberries
- 4 tbsp milk

Steps

1. In a medium mixing bowl, add butter, flour, sugar, and baking powder. mix until crumbly.
2. Add in the egg, milk, one tbsp at a time, until the dough forms. Stir in the blueberries.
3. Roll the dough, until it is 1.5cm thick. Cut with 5cm cutter into rounds.
4. Spray air fryer basket with cooking spray.
5. Put scones in air fryer basket in a single layer.
6. Cook at 380°F/195°C for 5-6 minutes, until golden.

Blueberry Hand Pies

Prep Time
15 Minutes

Cook Time
12 Minutes

Total Time
27 Minutes

Serving Size
8 servings

INGREDIENTS

- 125g fresh blueberries
- 3 tbsp caster sugar
- 1 tsp lemon juice
- 1 pinch salt
- 320g refrigerated pie crust or shortcrust pastry roll
- water

Steps

1. in a medium bowl, mix blueberries, sugar, lemon juice, and salt.
2. Roll out the piecrusts and cut out 6-8 10cm individual circles.
3. Place 1 tbsp of blueberry filling in center of each circle. Moisten edges of dough with water, and fold the dough over the filling to form a half moon shape. Using a fork, gently crimp the edges of the piecrust together.
4. Spray hand pies with cooking spray and sprinkle with sugar.
5. Preheat the air fryer to 350°F/180°C. Place 3-4 hand pies in single layer inside air fryer basket.
6. Cook for 12 mins until golden brown.
7. Let the pies cool for at least 10 mins before serving.

Super Moist Chocolate Cupcakes

- 100g unsweetened cocoa powder
- 125ml hot water
- 200g caster sugar
- 70ml oil
- 125ml milk
- 1 egg
- 1 tsp vanilla essence
- 120g flour
- 3/4 tsp baking powder
- 3/4 tsp baking soda
- 1/2 tsp salt

Chocolate Buttercream Icing:
- 8 tbsp butter, (softened)
- 225g icing sugar
- 3 tbsp cocoa powder
- 1/4 tsp vanilla essence
- 1 to 4 tbsp milk

Prep Time 20 Minutes **Cook Time** 12 Minutes **Total Time** 32 Minutes **Serving Size** 10 servings

Steps

1. Preheat the air fryer to 310°F/155°C.
2. Line 12 silicone cupcake holders with paper cupcake liners.
3. In a large bowl, add cocoa and hot water, mix until cocoa dissolved. Add sugar, oil, milk, egg, and vanilla . Whisk. Sift in flour, baking powder, baking soda, and salt and stir.
4. Divide the batter into cupcake holders and put them in air fryer basket.
5. Air fry for 12 minutes. Remove from air fryer and let cool.

Chocolate buttercream Icing:

1. Beat the butter until soft & creamy. Add icing sugar & cocoa. Beat until combined. Add salt & vanilla extract and beat. Slowly add milk and beat.
2. Spread on cooled cupcakes.

Cinnamon Rolls

Prep Time
15 *Minutes*

Cook Time
15 *Minutes*

Total Time
30 *Minutes*

Serving Size
6 *servings*

INGREDIENTS

For the rolls:
- 120g plain flour
- 4 tsp caster sugar
- 1 tsp baking powder
- 1/8 tsp baking soda
- 1/4 tsp salt
- 4 tbsp cold butter, cut into cubes
- 80ml milk

For the cinnamon filling:
- 2 tbsp melted butter
- 100g brown sugar
- 1 tsp ground cinnamon

Cream Cheese Icing:
- 4 tbsp soft cream cheese
- 1 tbsp soft butter
- 60g icing sugar
- 1/4 tsp vanilla essence
- 1 tsp milk (optional)

Steps

1. Preheat the air fryer to 320°F/160°C. Grease a 10-cm round cake tin.

2. In bowl, add flour, sugar, baking powder, baking soda, and salt. Mix. Add butter and mash it into the flour until it looks like sand. Add milk. Mix until form a dough. Transfer dough to floured surface and roll out into a 23x30cm rectangle.

3. Mix the cinnamon filling ingredients in a bowl. Spread the filling over the dough rectangle. Roll dough up into a log. Cut the log into 6 pieces and place them into prepared cake tin.

4. Put the tin into the air fryer basket and Air Fry for 14 minutes.

5. In a large bowl, add cream cheese filling ingredients. mix until combined.

6. Remove rolls from air fryer and drizzle the icing over the top.

Banana Souffle

Prep Time
15 Minutes

Cook Time
15 Minutes

Total Time
30 Minutes

Serving Size
6 servings

INGREDIENTS

- 2 ripe bananas
- 2 large eggs
- ½ tsp. cinnamon

Steps

1. In a blender, put the banana, eggs and cinnamon and blend until smooth.
2. Spray ramekins with cooking spray.
3. Divide the souffle batter into the ramekins & place them in the air fryer basket.
4. Air fry at 350°F / 180°C for 15 min.
5. When tome is up, remove. Serve immediately.

Spiced Sweet Potato Pie

Prep Time
5 Minutes

Cook Time
15 Minutes

Total Time
20 Minutes

Serving Size
12 servings

INGREDIENTS

Filling:
- 220g sweet potato mash
- 100g brown sugar
- 125g vegetable oil
- 130g double cream
- 2 eggs
- 1 tsp vanilla essence
- 2 tsp cinnamon
- ¼ tsp ginger
- ¼ tsp nutmeg
- pinch of cloves

Crust:
- pre-made pie crust

Steps

1. Preheat the air fryer to 300°F/180°C.
2. Press the pie dough into the bottom of 8-cm pie plates.
3. Place all of the filling ingredients in a bowl and mix until smooth and silky.
4. Divide the the filling among the pie plates and place them in the air fryer basket.
5. Air Fry for 15 minutes until pies are set and cooked through.
6. Serve topped with nuts.

Burnt Cream

Prep Time 20 Minutes
Cook Time 32 Minutes
Total Time 1 hour 52 minutes
Serving Size 5 servings

INGREDIENTS

- 6 egg yolks
- 6 tbsp sugar divided- 4 tbsp for custard, 2 tbsp for carmelizing
- 220g double cream
- 2 tsps vanilla essence
- 1 pinch salt

Steps

1. In a bowl, add egg yolks, 4 tbsp sugar, double cream, vanilla and salt.
2. Divide mixture evenly between 5-6 ramekins. Cover each tightly with tinfoil. (use tinfoil wrapped all the way around the ramekin.)
3. Place in air fryer and cook at 370°F/188°C for 32 minutes.
4. remove hot ramekins and set on a rack to cool.
5. Once completely cooled, cover with plastic wrap and chill for 1 hour or up to 2 days.
6. When ready to serve, top each ramekin with 1 tsp sugar and then heat for 2-3 minutes in oven to caramelize sugar. Let stand for a few mins before serving.

English Pound Cake

Prep Time 15 Minutes
Cook Time 35 Minutes
Total Time 50 Minutes
Serving Size 6 servings

INGREDIENTS

- 200g caster sugar
- 150g dried fruits
- 200g plain flour
- 125g softened butter
- 4 eggs
- 1 teaspoon baking powder
- Zest of one lemon

Steps

1. Preheat air fryer to 320°F/160°C.
2. In a large bowl, add butter and sugar, lemon zest and beat with a hand mixer until light and fluffy.
3. Add eggs and beat for 4 minutes until combined. Add flour and baking powder and beat until creamy.
4. Add the dried fruits and mix.
5. Pour the dough into the prepared tin and cover with tin foil. Air fry for 15 minutes
6. Open air fryer, remove tin foil. Air fry for more 15 minutes until a toothpick inserted in the center comes out clean.
7. Allow the cake to cool for 10 minutes. Remove from tin, transfer to a cooling rack.
8. Slice and serve with tea.

Shortbread Cookies

Prep Time
10 *Minutes*

Cook Time
8 *Minutes*

Total Time
18 *Minutes*

Serving Size
8 servings

INGREDIENTS

- 6 tbsp Butter
- 50g icing sugar
- 100g plain flour

Steps

1. In a large bowl, add butter and sugar and beat with a hand mixer until light and fluffy. Add flour and mix to combine. The dough would be crumbly, do not over mix. Use your hands to bring the dough together to form a ball.
2. Roll dough into a log. Wrap tightly in cling film and refrigerate for 30 mins.
3. Remove dough from the fridge, unwrap and slice into 1.5cm slices
4. Line air fryer basket with baking paper making sure there is at least 5cm of room round to ensure proper heat and air circulation.
5. Transfer cookies to air fryer basket and Air Fry at 330°F/166°C for 10 mins. Let cookies cool for 5 mins in the air fryer before transferring to a cooling rack with a cookie lifter to cool completely.

Oat Cookies

Prep Time
15 Minutes

Cook Time
15 Minutes

Total Time
30 Minutes

Serving Size
12 servings

INGREDIENTS

- 110g porridge oats
- 50g smooth peanut butter
- 200g unsweetened applesauce
- 35g dried fruits
- 25g dark chocolate chips

Steps

1. Line the air fryer basket with baking paper.
2. In a large bowl, mix all the ingredients until a dough is formed.
3. Divide the dough into 6 balls, pressing down to flatten (1cm thick).
4. Put 3 cookies in the fryer basket
5. Air Fry at 375°F/190°C. Repeat with remaining cookies.
6. Let cookies cool for 5 mins. Then serve.

Mini Lemon Cakes

Prep Time
20 Minutes

Cook Time
6 Minutes

Total Time
26 Minutes

Serving Size
12 servings

INGREDIENTS

- 2 eggs
- Juice & zest of 1 lemon
- 40g plain flour
- 60ml melted butter
- 70g caster sugar
- 125ml milk

Steps

1. Grease and flour mini muffin tins.
2. In a bowl, whisk all the ingredients until combined.
3. Divide the batter into prepared muffin tins. Put muffin tins in the air fryer basket.
4. Air fry for 6 mins at 320°F/160°C.
5. Remove from air fryer, Let cool for 5 mins. Then serve.

Blackberry Crisp

Prep Time 10 Minutes | Cook Time 10 Minutes | Total Time 20 Minutes | Serving Size 3 servings

INGREDIENTS

Filling:
- 200g fresh blackberries
- 50g caster sugar
- 50g brown sugar
- 1/3 cup flour
- 1 tbsp lemon juice

Topping :
- 120g Instant Oatmeal
- 120g flour
- 150g brown sugar
- 1 teaspoon salt
- 200g butter

Steps

1. In a bowl, add blackberries, sugars, flour and lemon juice, and sugar. Let it sit for about 10 mins. Then add the blackberries to a greased 3 ramekin.
2. In a bowl, mix Instant Oatmeal , flour, brown sugar, salt, and butter. Then sprinkle evenly over blackberries mixture.
3. Air Fry at 166°C/330°F for 8 mins.
4. Remove once golden on top, let cool slightly then serve with ice cream.

Apple Pie Pastries

Prep Time 5 Minutes | Cook Time 45 Minutes | Total Time 50 Minutes | Serving Size 6 servings

INGREDIENTS

- 3 apples, peeled & finely diced
- 1 tbsp lemon juice
- 2 tsp plain flour
- 2 tsp cinnamon
- 2 tsp brown sugar
- 1/2 tsp nutmeg
- 1/2 tsp ground cloves
- 10 sheets filo pastry
- 170g melted butter

Steps

1. In bowl, add all ingredients except filo pastry. Mix.
2. Place one filo sheet on a large piece of baking paper, brush with butter. Put 6 tbsp apple filling in the middle of the filo. Roll up the sheet stopping once or twice to brush the pastry with butter. Once done, brush all over with butter. repeat with remaining filo pastry.
3. Air fry at 320°F/160°C for 6 minutes.
4. Remove from air fryer. Allow to cool slightly before serving.

12727518R00045